Penguin Books
The Seventh Gate

'Leper at Large on Liner.' That was the headline in the
News of the World, which heralded the arrival in
England of Peter Greave.

He had come for treatment to a small hospital in Essex,
run by an order of Anglican nuns, and it was during his
stay with this small community that he met a young
novice who resigned her novitiate in order to become his
wife.

Peter Greave was the author of two plays, and gave many
unscripted talks for the B.B.C. In spite of increasing
disability and, finally, blindness, he wrote several
books which belied his ill-health, and show a wry sense of
humour, as well as a great insight into the under-belly
of India where he spent his youth.

He continued to write books at The Homes of St
Giles, in Essex, where he lived until his death in
November 1977.

His books include *The Second Miracle*, *Young Man in
the Sun* and *The Painted Leopard*.

Peter Greave

The Seventh Gate

Penguin Books

Penguin Books Ltd, Harmondsworth,
Middlesex, England
Penguin Books, 625 Madison Avenue,
New York, New York 10022, U.S.A.
Penguin Books Australia Ltd, Ringwood,
Victoria, Australia
Penguin Books Canada Ltd, 2801 John Street,
Markham, Ontario, Canada L3R 1B4
Penguin Books (N.Z.) Ltd, 182–190 Wairau Road,
Auckland 10, New Zealand

First published by Maurice Temple Smith Ltd, 1976
Published in Penguin Books 1978

Made and printed in Great Britain by
Hazell Watson & Viney Ltd, Aylesbury, Bucks
Set in Linotype Plantin

This book is dedicated to Sandra Clancy, with affection and gratitude, in remembrance of all the long hours she spent recording my slow, clumsy sentences.

It is also written for my friend David, who has striven so successfully to use his eyes and hands on my behalf.

'*He who enters the Seventh Gate*
may not retrace his footsteps.'

I

I was sixty-three on my last birthday; not very old, but old enough, and when I remember all that those years conceal, I can't help but feel a sort of rueful pride at having survived for so long. God knows there have been dark times, but now, looking back, I realize that they were not really important; not at least, in comparison to all those other years, so rich in love, friendship and adventure, which were the more satisfying because they were achieved when I was living on borrowed time.

Now I sit on the side of my bed, wearing crumpled pyjamas, a thin, old man, with grey hair and a battered face that makes me look like a worn-out boxer who has been at the wrong end of too many punches, and I strive to focus my mind on the past. I sit here, engulfed in a grey, opaque mist, in this silent room, deep in the placid English countryside, and the ghosts of the past, the dazzling Indian sunlight, and a thousand half-remembered faces drift through my mind; and the task of capturing these blurred memories seems almost impossible. There is so much to remember: love, pain, terror, joy, the long wandering years, so many ultimates of human experience.

Even with a whole book to fill, it will be necessary to exclude vast areas of my life, or, at the best, touch on them so lightly that much of their significance must be lost. Lurking behind these pages are the phantoms of half a dozen other unwritten books which my readers must detect for themselves. It is almost certain that I shall not have the time to write them, and so this record, with all its imperfections and omissions, must serve as best it can.

I was born in Calcutta on the twenty-ninth of October 1910. My mother had been taken to the Medical College Hospital for the confinement, and according to the family legend, soon after I had emerged, the old Brahmin doctor presiding over the operation bent forward and felt the shape of my infant skull with his long brown fingers; he is then supposed to have murmured thoughtfully, 'This one will be a wanderer,' and if this is so, it was not a bad guess. I have indeed been a wanderer, a nomad, for a great part of my life, and an insatiable curiosity, which operates on both the physical and mental level, has compelled me to follow each unknown turning, knock on every closed door, and never reject an untried experience.

In those days, my parents, my brother Michael and I lived in a large, comfortable old house, isolated from the world outside by a high wall, and a tall, green gate. It was a peaceful, spacious house, topped by a terrace and fronted by a massive portico with yellow pillars. It stood in the centre of a large garden ablaze with the colours of tropical flowers, which included a small circular lake, as green as jade. The house itself, with its airy rooms and long open veranda, radiated peace and comfort, and to this day, when I think of home, my mind returns to that lost, beautiful domain which for a few years offered a happiness and security that I was never to experience again. We lived in an expensive European suburb of the city, known then, and perhaps still, as Ballygunge, and in these surroundings, the noisy, crowded bazaars seemed to belong to a different dimension.

All I knew were days of fierce sunlight, and nights of hot, velvet darkness, punctuated by the distant sound of bugle calls from the Indian cavalry lines half a mile away. Every evening, when the worst of the heat was over, we were taken for a walk by our Anglo-Indian nanny. Scrubbed and neat, and slightly subdued, we walked on either side of her, past other large, mysterious houses, exactly as though we were pretending to be a couple of real little English boys promenading across Hampstead Heath.

I have said that this was a period of innocence, but that is not strictly accurate. Even then I was conscious that this apparent serenity concealed a shadow of danger and uncertainty. I must have picked up hints of this in various ways, but I can remember only one. After supper we were taken upstairs and prepared for bed, and then, kneeling together in our pyjamas, we would recite our prayers supervised by our nurse. On several occasions she interrupted us by saying, apparently without reason, 'Don't forget to pray for your father and to ask God's mercy on him.' This was said in such a sombre tone of voice that it left me with a deep sense of disquiet, which was the more disturbing because I was quite unable to think of any reason why my father should be in special need of prayer or mercy. It seems strange to recall that it never occurred to me to report these incidents to my mother.

My earliest memory of myself as a separate and recognizable personality dates back to a time when I was about four years old. I must, in some way, have escaped from the house and strayed deep into the garden entirely on my own. It was early morning, and though the garden was bathed in dazzling sunshine, the air was comparatively cool. Trotting happily forward on my diminutive legs, I wandered on and on, until at last I reached the high wall that marked the limits of my world. For the first time in my life I was completely alone, free from the restraining pressures of adult authority, and this knowledge filled me with a strange, intoxicating happiness that was like nothing I had ever known before. Now I belonged to myself, unobserved, unfettered, and all around me was the fantastic beauty of the unknown. This sense of release and joy was so powerful that I can still remember it distinctly, and it was an intimation of certain deeply rooted traits that were later to shape the entire course of my life.

I stood still, glancing around me with eager curiosity. I was so small that the shrubbery reached high above my head, leaving me engulfed in a haze of dim, cool light. A large butterfly, with turquoise-coloured wings, almost touched my shoulder as it fluttered past, a villainous black crow alighted on a branch, turning its head from side to side. Far behind me I could hear the murmur of the servants' voices from their quarters a hundred yards away. I was overwhelmed by the mysterious beauty of this entrancing world. And then, suddenly, from the undergrowth at the base of the wall, something black, swift and evil darted towards me. I could not have understood the extremity of my peril, but the sight of this creature, with its great swollen head swaying rhythmically as it slithered forward in a series of sinuous curves, instantly warned me that I was in danger.

I stood absolutely still, and for the second time that morning, within the space of a few minutes, I had my first experience of yet another adventure of the soul. I was gripped by terror: its dark power numbed my body. The cobra paused directly in front of me. Though no longer advancing, its body was in constant motion, weaving complicated, graceful designs as it swayed and circled with a perfection of balance and speed. It reared upward, so that its eyes and its black, forked tongue were within a few inches of my face. It swung backward, prepared to strike; but at that exact second the crow perched on the branch above us suddenly opened its wings and took to flight. The cobra's hooded head flashed round to follow the sound, and then its long, deadly body sank downwards, and with swift, convulsive movements it made off through the bushes.

I started to cry, the tears streaming down my cheeks. I must have stood like that for a couple of minutes, and then, from somewhere near the house came the sound of running feet, and thudding blows. Soon afterwards, one of the servants appeared, took my hand, and led me away. Half a dozen Indians stood in a circle, talking excitedly, as they stared down at something limp and battered that lay on the gravel in front of the stables. I joined the group of laughing, chattering men, and an instant later, with an odd mixture of compassion and distaste, was looking down at all that was left of that unexpected encounter. That once swift, proud fugitive was now a mass of blood and pulp lying on the pebbles.

I learnt, eventually, that it was a king cobra, just under five feet in length; and perhaps I should add that in all my thirty-three years in India this was the only occasion I ever came into close proximity with a poisonous snake. I was to remember that eventful morning for the rest of my life, probably because it was totally unlike the ordered innocence of those carefree early years. My brother and I played endlessly together in that wild, beautiful garden, listened to my mother telling us fairy stories, enjoying a world that seemed filled with little that was not pleasurable and exciting. I suppose I could say that this period represented all I was ever to know of the innocence that once existed in that other legendary garden.

Those were the days when the British Raj seemed as impregnable as a mountain range, and if anybody had prophesied that within four short decades the Union Jack would no longer flutter over Government House, and that the last British bayonet was doomed to disappear, they would only have provoked scornful laughter.

My father would certainly have shared in this mirth. At that time (and I am writing now of the years between 1910 and 1914) his career was approaching its zenith, and he had every right to expect prolonged and increasing success. He was a tall, good-looking man, talkative and assured, as quick and light on his feet as a boxer. His jet black hair grew to a point above a straight, commanding nose, and his jaw was firm and pugnacious. His worst feature was his mouth, the lips thick and a little cruel, and in his eyes there was an odd, baffled expression, as though he were constantly at war with something inside himself. I was barely conscious of his existence in those early days, but sometimes his tall figure, immaculate in tussore silk, would flash through the house, talking loudly, rapping out orders, leaving a trail of excitement and noise behind him. He was a strange, unpredictable character with many tastes that were far from desirable, and his influence on our lives was so destructive that I find it difficult to write about him dispassionately. It would be useless to attempt to disguise the flaws and eccentricity that were a part of his personality, but at the same time it is only fair to say that he was one of the most courageous men I have ever met, capable of displaying both generosity and understanding at the most unlikely moments. He was a big man in every sense and, in his fashion, he remained true to himself to the end. I think that he found little in me to admire, and yet it is a fact that during the entire course of my childhood, and for many years afterwards, I sought to win his praise in every way possible, although I was seldom successful. But as his personality, and the turbulent pattern of his life, were destined to influence all that follows, I had better write of him now at some length.

2

My father was born in Manchester, and I suppose his family could roughly be classified as middle class. They were certainly a very odd tribe indeed; a little mad, and more than a little bad, and though my father seldom spoke of them, the few facts that did emerge produced in me a distaste for the inhabitants of that city that survives even now. They seemed to me to be both intolerant and violent, and from an early age I mentally disowned them and allied myself to my mother's Irish forbears. However, despite his Manchester upbringing and exaggerated English prejudices, my father's mother was also Irish. Her maiden name was Karen O'Grady, and she had met my grandfather somewhere east of Suez in circumstances that are still mysterious. I imagine that socially she was slightly superior to her husband, as her father had been a Captain commanding, of all things, an Elephant Battery in the forces of the East India Company.

I know almost nothing of Karen O'Grady myself, though vague family legends indicate that her morals and her tastes were well in advance of her time. I still possess a faded photograph of her, taken, I suppose, about eighty years ago, and there is something about her appearance that suggests a self-willed arrogance that boded little comfort for her spouse. My grandfather was employed by an organization known as the Eastern Telegraph Company, which operated throughout the East, and apparently his duties forced him to spend many years in Aden, which in those days must have been a hell-hole indeed. I know that the couple, plus their small son, my father, spent several years together in this rocky, sun-scorched wilderness, and that their life together was abruptly terminated by the mysterious death of my grandfather.

I have no idea how he died, and my father always remained singularly reticent when the subject arose. It might have been suicide, the onslaught of a tropical disease, an excess of whisky or possibly a fatal accident. But certain facts are beyond dispute: Karen O'Grady left her husband and deserted her small son at a time when he could not have been much more than four years old. This child, my father, was eventually returned to England, and placed in the care of his uncle in Manchester. His childhood must have been far from happy, and I think that even in those early days he displayed a reckless disregard for the opinions and wishes of a family that must have looked upon him as an undeserved encumbrance.

Nevertheless, his intelligence and good looks got him out of many scrapes, and in due course he was sent to Manchester Grammar School. He did fairly well at his studies, though I am sure that he did not particularly enjoy his schooling, and it was probably a relief when, at the age of sixteen, his uncle decided to withdraw him. Exactly as his father before him, he was offered a post by the Eastern Telegraph Company, and started work by mastering morse code and learning to operate the machines then used to despatch cables across the world. No doubt his relatives now believed that he was settled for life, but if so they were soon to be disillusioned. In less than a year he was sacked with ignominy and found himself wandering the streets, pondering how to face his uncle with such disastrous news.

I do not know, and no doubt will never know, what he had done to justify such drastic reprisals, although I can make a guess in the light of certain facts about my father which will become clear later. But what followed appears to be simple enough. Dusk was falling as he prowled through the city, trying to find courage to return home and confront his uncle. The lights were lit, he was jostled by the passing crowd, the trams jangled and clattered, hansom cabs sped past, and still his feet carried him forward aimlessly. Suddenly he knew that, whatever the consequences, he could not face the ordeal of explaining what had happened and consequently it was impossible for him ever to return home. The year was 1900, and the Boer War continued to drag on. He noticed a poster on the front of a warehouse. In large black letters it told him to fight for his Queen and his Country, and at that moment this crude invocation seemed the answer to a prayer.

He walked firmly and rapidly now, because he had an objective, a possible solution to all his difficulties. Within a minute or two, he had made his way to a recruiting centre. He walked in and found himself confronting a grizzled Sergeant-major, whose welcoming smile changed rapidly to an expression of distrust as he scanned the boy standing before him. When he heard that my father wanted to join the army, he shook his head impatiently, and snorted, 'You, join the Army? Not bloody likely: you go back to school, sonny, and leave men to fight the war.'

'I was twenty-one two months ago,' my father lied, with that effrontery which he was to display so often in later years, and there was silence for a minute as the man studied him thoughtfully.

'You're on the run, my boy,' he said accusingly, and then thought for a moment before adding, 'But if you want to get killed, it's none of my business.' Twenty seconds later the boy had accepted the Queen's shilling and signed a form which testified that he was over twenty-one.

Being, even then, big and strong and nearly six feet tall, he was put into a Guards regiment, and six months later was on a troopship bound for the Cape. His regiment remained in Africa for over a year, but according to what I heard later, he did little fighting, and hardly ever saw a Boer at close quarters. I am sure that my father made a deplorable soldier, and everything he said later indicated that he was constantly running foul of military discipline. He was charged with over-staying his leave, with dumb insolence, with refusing to obey the orders of his superior officers, damaging government property, and a dozen other misdeeds. I don't think that the officers, or the men, knew exactly what to make of him, except that everybody appeared to agree that he was a complete liability to this or any other army.

Early in 1902, when he had still to reach his nineteenth birthday, the regiment was ordered to India. They landed at Bombay, and after a few weeks went on to Agra where they settled to a long period of peace-time duties. And now my father, in some extraordinary fashion, managed to raise the money to buy himself out of the army. It appears that he had a cousin who had entered the Church of England, and he seems to have written to this guileless priest and to have succeeded in extracting whatever sum was required to allow him to return to civilian life. I am certain that his escape from the army represented a particularly happy point in his career. There he was, not yet nineteen, bursting with strength and confidence, and all around him, like an oyster waiting to be opened, lay the vast expanse of India.

From then on the improvement in his fortunes can only be described as spectacular. Within the space of six years, the young ex-cavalry trooper who had landed in Bombay with nothing except a couple of pounds and the contents of his kit-bag, had blossomed into a minor commercial magnate living in comparative luxury in Calcutta. He owned an enormous grey Berliot car, which rattled ferociously immediately the engine was started, and a black Arab horse named Kismet, and he occupied an expensive flat in Theatre Road. His car, which was probably among the first few motor vehicles to reach Calcutta, was to remain in his possession for many years; I remember distinctly that it was always enveloped in an overpowering smell of petrol, and that whenever it rained everyone had to leap out and struggle frantically to erect its canvas hood. Sitting at the wheel of this Juggernaut, my father drove at breakneck speed across the city, cackling chickens and bleating goats flying from his path, while the tall, dignified Sikh chauffeur sitting beside him watched the road and his master with nervous distaste.

Obviously pure luck had something to do with this sudden leap towards affluence, but I am sure most of it was the product of his extraordinary originality and enterprise. In those days the commercial life of Bengal was still influenced by the traditions of the East India Company, which meant that everything was done at a leisurely, dignified pace. The great European mercantile firms were housed in huge, rambling offices occupied by hundreds of *babu* clerks scribbling apathetically in the ledgers, while the godlike sahibs seldom presented themselves for work before 10.30 in the morning and left soon after five in the evening. It was simply not done to display speed or enthusiasm, and the policy of compromise and inertia was generally apparent. My father's explosive energy must have shattered this stagnation, and it is hardly surprising that he was able to achieve rapid success.

Soon after leaving the army he managed to secure an insignificant post in a small business that specialized in the timber trade. The manager of this company was a Welshman named Evans, and it appears that the fortunes of the business were at a particularly low ebb. In less than a year the personality of his new assistant brought a transfusion of new life into what had seemed a dying organization. The young man discovered new sources of profit and travelled all over the country negotiating lucrative contracts in ways which the older man hardly knew existed. The great Indian railway companies were expanding, and this new recruit travelled as far afield as Gwalior and Hyderabad to obtain orders for hundreds of thousands of sleepers from the native states. Within a couple of years he had taken control of the business, and was soon earning very considerable sums indeed.

I do not think he was particularly liked by his contemporaries, and it seems astonishing that an unknown ex-cavalry man should have gained acceptance from the hidebound establishment that ruled India at that time. But, in fact, he did succeed in penetrating those hallowed circles, joined two ultra-snobbish clubs, and became a member of the Calcutta Light Horse which prided itself on excluding practically everyone except the residents of Government House. If he worked hard, he certainly played with no less energy. He bought himself a beautiful Kashmiri girl, fair-skinned and blue-eyed, and installed her in his flat, though I am sure that he was hardly conscious of her existence. A number of women must have attempted to trap him, but though he was involved in numerous affairs, he was able to avoid matrimony.

And then, one night, at a dance, he saw a tall, slim girl with dark hair and instantly fell in love. He discovered that her name was Katherine Tighe, that she was Irish, and that her father, who had died a few years earlier, had been Assistant Commissioner of Police in Bombay. Katherine had been engaged for two years to a man who was deeply devoted to her, but within three months of her introduction to my father, this engagement was broken, and she had agreed to marry this unknown Englishman. At this stage my father was offered a job by Doyle & Company, one of the leading firms in the city; he became the manager of their timber department, earning a large salary and a ten per cent commission on the contracts he obtained. Everything suggested that he was well on the way to a secure and successful life, and consequently he rented a comfortable house, and was married to my mother according to the rites of the Catholic Church. The young couple spent their honeymoon in Kashmir, and after an appropriate time their first child was born and christened Peter.

My mother, in her simplicity and strength, represented a complete contrast to the incalculable, restless personality of my father. She was a fervent, though unusually broad-minded Roman Catholic, the product of a home which was both happy and secure. Her father, an Irishman from Connaught, had never failed to accept the responsibilities of a husband and father, and consequently her early life had been surrounded by a stability and innocence which was instantly discernible. Her temperament was instinctively happy and tranquil, and she had the capacity to be content under almost any circumstances. All she desired from life was a certain permanence, a home that she could call her own and the opportunity to care for her children; but she was never destined to achieve even these simple ambitions. I suppose that, had she searched the entire world, she could hardly have found a man less likely to make her happy than my father, and yet it never occurred to her to desert him in spite of the havoc he was to make of their joint lives. He brought her nothing but misery and disgrace, but even so, her loyalty to him never faltered.

3

My life in the big house, surrounded by that sun-drenched garden, was soon to end. My parents left India on a prolonged business trip that took them first to England and then, after many difficulties, right across Europe into south Russia. The big, old house was closed down, and my brother and I were sent to Darjeeling, a small hill-station perched half-way up the Himalayas, in the charge of an Anglo-Indian nurse and a young Indian *ayah*. It appeared that my father, whose commercial career had reached its zenith, had been sent by Doyle & Company to negotiate the purchase of large consignments of railway sleepers in Odessa. The 1914 war was on and these supplies were both difficult to get and urgently needed.

It seems difficult to understand how my mother, who was certainly acutely conscious of her responsibility as a parent, could justify this separation from two small boys, and I did not glimpse the answer to this puzzle until I was much older. I realized then that she was probably so troubled and confused by her husband's extraordinary temperament that she was afraid to let him out of her sight for a single avoidable moment. I am sure that she left my brother and me with reluctance and deep misgiving, but I suppose that at the time this seemed the only possible solution. Once removed from that sunlit garden and all that had represented security and happiness, I found myself confronted with some of the fears and uncertainties which were to become only too familiar.

In Darjeeling the four of us, that is, our nurse, the young Indian *ayah*, my brother and myself, occupied a small, white bungalow standing half-way down the mountain slope. A hundred yards above it was a flat stretch of land, scooped from the flank of the mountain, and on it stood a Roman Catholic convent with its own nursery school, which later enrolled my brother and myself. In theory at least, we were supposed to be under the supervision of the nuns, but events proved that they were completely useless in this role. Within a matter of days I was to learn for the first time that existence could be both painful and treacherous.

We called our nurse Sophie; I cannot now remember her surname, and my memories of her are fragmented and indistinct. This is a little surprising, because it seems certain that this woman's influence on my life was profoundly destructive. Sophie was tall and unusually dark for an Anglo-Indian, with the flat nose and thick lips that might have been due to traces of African blood. She had a long, muscular neck, heavy-lidded eyes, and her fleshy lips were slightly purple. She generally wore a white blouse and a long, dark skirt, and her hair, black as ink, was arranged in coils round her head. I have never been in a position to judge either her motives or her temperament, but it is clear that she chose to ill-treat me systematically over a period of many months. I would frequently appear with cuts and bruises on my arms and back, the result apparently of fairly savage beatings with a long hairbrush.

I suspect that these thrashings expressed some kind of sexual element, and can only conclude that I was used as the target for a sadistic appetite. I feel certain now, however improbable this may sound, that our relationship was based on some form of bizarre sexuality, and it is an extraordinary fact that neither then nor later was I aware of the least resentment towards her. I must have been an extremely tough little boy, because it was eventually disclosed that I was often bruised all over the body, and also that the nuns had observed my battered condition on several occasions. However, instead of immediately reporting what they had seen to my mother, these soft-hearted religious cretins decided to display the virtues of charity at my expense. I heard later that when Sophie was confronted by the evidence of her neglect and cruelty, she would burst into a flood of tears, swear to mend her ways, and assure the credulous sisters that she would hurry to confession the next morning and be absolved from her sins. Soothed by these assurances, the nuns decided that it was best in everyone's interest to conceal the facts from my parents.

The odd part is that my brother Michael was excluded from these sadistic attentions, and I am still unable to understand the reason for this immunity. I think that I was an unusually affectionate, responsive child, and possibly this guileless quality appealed to Sophie's special tastes more than my brother's aloof, restrained character.

But our life in Darjeeling produced other experiences of a far happier kind. The mountainous countryside offered so many wonders to enchant the mind of a small boy. Great peaks soared into the sky, overlooking deep sunless valleys covered in jungle. Far away to the north the snow-capped pinnacle of Mount Everest gleamed like a phantom against the clear, cold sky. Everything was bathed in delicate, translucent sunlight, quite unlike the dazzling savagery of the light in the plains. The hillside teemed with strange plants and animals. Enormous butterflies flitted through the air, there were ferns and wild flowers in profusion and mountain streams gushing through the rocks.

Everything in Darjeeling was either high or low, so that one was constantly scrambling upwards, or rapidly descending. Towards evening it became very cold, and blankets of mist, like vast clouds of smoke, obliterated the landscape. After nightfall the bazaar glittered with hundreds of tiny lights, and inside the dark shops Tibetans and the other hill-people offered turquoise necklaces and richly woven blankets to the passers-by. As the night advanced, troops of hungry jackals howled in chorus just outside the town. And, of course, there were the less pleasing aspects of Himalayan life that could not be ignored. The hillsides, over-grown with tropical foliage, were infested with leeches which clung to the legs and knees of anyone who trespassed through their domain. When it rained, it came down in a clammy deluge, and on other occasions hailstones, the size of marbles, dropped out of the sky.

It was a fascinating world for a child, but more than anything else I enjoyed riding the small, wiry pony that was brought to my door two or three times every week. These ponies were re-ferred to as 'tats', and were always controlled by diminutive Bhutia boys capable of following a galloping pony with extra-ordinary ease. Like everyone else I soon developed a real affection and respect for the hill people. Their yellow, Mongolian faces radiated happiness, while their stocky, muscular bodies were able to endure unbelievable exertions and privations. I loved my pony with passionate intensity, and can still recall the delightful odour of sweat and leather exuded by his powerful brown body. Moun-ted on this animal, trotting happily down the track that led away from the town, I experienced moments of extreme content. Within a few minutes, the convent, Sophie, and all my other problems were left behind, and I was conscious of a sensation of utter freedom. A kind of friendship soon developed between me and my pony-boy, a youth of about twelve, with long, dark hair, and inscrutable black eyes. He would offer me cheap bazaar ciga-rettes, which we would share in complete amity, immediately we reached a point of comparative safety.

Soon after our arrival in Darjeeling, my brother and I were enrolled in the kindergarten run by the Roman Catholic Sisters. My initial experience of life among my contemporaries was shat-tering. As I approached the school on that first morning, the door suddenly opened and a horde of squealing girls and boys rushed out to meet me. In a second I was surrounded by a circle of children, all of whom instantly proceeded to prod and jostle me, while they all yelped, 'Kaiser Bill, Kaiser Bill,' prancing round me with demoniac glee. I was completely confused, totally incapable of understanding their hostility. And then, as the group continued to swirl round me, I suddenly spotted the fat pink face of a little boy of about my own age. Instinctively, I doubled my fist, drew back my puny arm, and struck my tormentor straight in the eye. There was a sudden silence, and almost instantly the attack was over; I had learnt my first practical lesson in coping with the problems of life.

My feelings about school were relatively neutral; I didn't like it, but I didn't particularly dislike it. One point is certain, I was not a very bright scholar, and when some problem was proffered to the class almost everyone seemed to find the answer before I did. I was probably what would now be described as a slow developer, but in those forthright days the term used was 'stupid'.

My brother Michael was undoubtedly a great deal more successful in an academic sense than I. He was also much more capable of winning the esteem of the adult world than I could ever be. His temperament and outlook even then were completely unlike my own. He could remain detached from his surroundings, while I was always emotionally involved with events and people. My reactions to life were instinctively happy and optimistic, while his nature veered towards distrust and pessimism. Sophie never attempted to ill-treat him, and most of the adults with whom we came in contact were instantly predisposed in his favour. We were never very close, and when I was being beaten by Sophie he would stand watching the scene with indifference. Nevertheless, in spite of his good looks and intelligence, he was then, and later, inferior in anything that demanded physical enterprise. His coordination was slow, and he could never be persuaded to mount a pony, or to scramble down the steep rocks with which the country abounded. The odd part is that I never envied his apparent superiority, but accepted this as a fact of life.

Very soon the memory of my tall, beautiful mother became hardly more than a dream. My world consisted of the incalculable Sophie, the vague presence of the nuns; and all I could do was to strive for survival in surroundings that constantly confronted me with pressures and ordeals that were totally beyond my comprehension. And yet, mother must have gone to considerable trouble to ensure that she was not forgotten. Every day, over a period of many months, the Indian postman delivered a brightly coloured postcard from her, despatched from London, Marseilles, Rome and finally Russia. She would write brief, affectionate messages on these cards, which we collected in a large album. But somehow these tenuous contacts with what had once seemed so important did little to encourage me. I was still very young when I learnt that the basic condition of human existence was injustice and insecurity.

My torments at the hands of the sadistic Sophie came to a head one wet afternoon about six months after we had come to Darjeeling. We were on the veranda, and she was laying into me with unusual ferocity, using her favourite weapon, the long-handled hairbrush. I can remember the dismal pattering of the falling rain, the smell of wet earth that drifted in from the garden, and incongruously, a large empty wooden box that was probably a discarded tea-chest. I do not know what crime I was supposed to have committed, and perhaps by this time even the pretence of justification had been dropped, but the woman seemed intoxicated by the desire to inflict pain. My small naked bottom pointed upward, her fingers clutched my neck, forcing my head towards the floor, and her right arm rose and fell as she rained a succession of savage blows on my unfortunate stern.

My recollection of those few frenzied seconds is extraordinarily distinct; I can still feel the weight of her hand as it gripped my neck, and the agonizing impact of the brush. My reactions should surely have been a mixture of acute terror and dismay, but instead what remains in my memory, alongside the sheer physical pain, is a curious sense of pleasure and excitement. If this is so, then Sophie's sustained cruelty must be considered in a new light. It may well be that I was not just a victim but also in a sense a participant in a ritual.

This scene was suddenly brought to an abrupt and unexpected conclusion. As the struggle reached its climax, I either lost my balance or was pushed downwards, and consequently fell forward, striking my chin on the point of a rusty nail protruding from the empty box already mentioned. I must have fallen with considerable force, because the blood instantly started to pour from a gash below my chin, and as the floor became slippery with the gruesome stuff, I really became frightened and emitted a loud terrified wail. Now came the repercussions, which were both rapid and dramatic. Two nuns appeared, and when they saw my condition numerous additional members of the Convent staff joined the audience. Sophie was obviously very frightened, and strove to explain incoherently that it was all an accident. But her earlier record, and the damning evidence of the hairbrush, which still lay on the floor smeared with blood, left no doubt as to the facts. I continued to bleed with uncontrollable enthusiasm and soon everything round me was splattered with ugly drops.

Finally, a rickshaw was summoned, and I was first bundled into a raincoat, and then hurried aboard this vehicle, accompanied by Sophie. Despite the efforts of four coolies, pushing us along at considerable speed, it took us nearly half an hour to reach the local hospital. Once there I was examined by an impassive Bhutia doctor, who embarrassed everyone by asking repeatedly in broken English, 'Wherefore is this this boy so hurted?', which was a question neither Sophie nor I was anxious to answer. Eventually I was stretched out flat on an operating table and the doctor, with great skill and without an anaesthetic, proceeded to use sixteen stitches to sew up my chin. I bore this ordeal reasonably well, and when it was over the kindly doctor not only praised my stoicism quite extravagantly, but also presented me with a large bar of chocolate which I managed to consume on our homeward journey.

Nothing much was said to me directly about this incident, but I know that it created a furore amongst the Sisters. Sophie was threatened with the severest reprisals, including a visit from the local police, which undoubtedly left her deeply shaken. I was not beaten again, and I think that from that moment a change took place in our relationship which was never the same again. Yet it may be worth recording that, even then, the good Sisters either avoided reporting this incident to my parents, or considered it unnecessary to do so. I had forgotten all about it within a matter of hours, but the scar left by that wound was to remain for the rest of my life. When I try to recall exactly what occurred during the course of the next few days, my memory becomes an unreliable instrument. Sophie, sullen and tearful, took to her bed, complaining of some imaginary illness, while I, to the best of my knowledge, was left mainly to my own devices. I did not feel that I had been ill-treated or harshly used, but was conscious instead of a blurred sensation of guilt which half convinced me that I was somehow to blame for all that had happened. The school was closed for the summer holidays, so I must have had ample time to think and remember, but I suspect that all I actually did was to retreat even deeper into my private world.

Several days must have passed in this way, and then came the morning which was to bring me moments of pure and unexpected happiness. The time must have been about 11 a.m., and my brother and I, bedraggled and forlorn, were playing on the hillside a dozen feet below the path that led to our cottage. For some reason, my recollection of what then ensued still survives sharp and clear, like the picture on the screen of a defective television which is suddenly attuned correctly. Wearing a dirty blue jersey, with my chin still covered with a bandage that had not been changed for days, I stood gazing aimlessly towards the far horizon. A short distance below me, my brother was squatting on his hunkers, his pale, thin face expressing the strange absorption of childhood. Heaven knows what we were supposed to be doing, but I do know that although we were physically close, both of us were immersed in fantasies that were strictly private.

A faint sound brought my head round, and there, standing on the path above me, was a tall, beautiful woman, half-smiling as she looked down at us. I remember staring at her in startled confusion. She seemed so young and attractive and was dressed with such sophisticated splendour that I could only look at her with inane concentration. And then she spoke, and the sound of her voice was vaguely familiar, though I was still too amazed to recognize my mother. She said gently, chidingly, 'Hello Peter, don't you remember me?' When I remained silent, she added quickly, 'What's happened to your chin?' And then, 'Where is Sophie?' I told her that Sophie was ill in bed, and by now my heart was hammering with happy anticipation, as my mind accustomed itself to this magnificent climax. She came down the hillside, and took us by the hand. As we walked towards the cottage, the words that I had repressed for so long came tumbling out. I didn't say anything about the beatings, but when she asked whether Sophie was often ill, I said 'Yes', and when she probed further and enquired why the *ayah* was also absent, I replied gleefully 'Oh, she's looking after Sophie.'

I don't think my mother needed more than a couple of minutes to get a fairly accurate picture of all that had been going on. Her face was unusually serious as we entered the cottage, and my brother and I were told to wait on the veranda while she entered the bedroom to confront Sophie. We could not clearly hear the conversation that followed, but there was a biting edge to her voice which left me in no doubt of the emotions that lay behind the words.

By the time she emerged, I knew that from now on my world had changed, and that everything was going to return to those old, joyful days before we had been forced to explore the unknown. After we had washed and changed into fresh clothes, Mother took us both back to her hotel some distance from the convent. Once inside her room we all surrendered to a mood of almost hysterical happiness. I felt as though I had escaped from a nightmare, and the room, crowded with her luggage, and strewn with her dresses and furs, was an enchanting assurance of a pattern of existence that I had almost forgotten. The following morning, after what must have been a somewhat bitter exchange between my mother and the nuns, the three of us boarded the train. Early the next day we were back in Calcutta.

4

My father and the big grey Berliot were waiting for us at Sealdah Station. Behind the wheel sat the smiling young Sikh, Lalsing, whom I remembered so well from what now seemed the distant past. The three of us climbed into its vast rear seat, and after frantic efforts with the starting handle, the engine roared into life and we were on our way home under lowering skies. After the clear, cool air of the mountains the heat of the city closed around us with suffocating force, and the filth and the smells of the bazaar were depressingly obvious. As always, the journey through the congested Bengali quarter, swarming with thousands of brown, alien faces all expressing veiled hostility towards the strangers in their midst, left me a little uneasy, but the certainty that I was returning home was so wonderful that I was hardly conscious of my surroundings. Three miles beyond the station, a monsoon storm burst and as the rain poured down on us the car was brought to a standstill, while my father and the driver, cursing and sweating, managed to haul the cumbersome canvas hood into place. But at last it was all over, and we were driving through the familiar iron gate and were in sight of the big, old, peaceful house with its welcoming portico, supported by tall yellow pillars.

Nothing had changed: there was the flight of white stone steps that led into the hall, and further on the staircase with the teak handrails that led to the upper landing, and brought one face t face with a large reproduction of an oil painting entitled, such was the simplicity of that era, *The Sale of Old Dobbin*. This picture represented a rather unlikely English farmyard, in which stood a large melancholy horse, which was being sold by its tearful owner. Beside the landing was the enormous living room opening onto a veranda running the entire length of the house. I stood on the veranda, and looked down at the garden, which seemed enormous to me then, drinking in the gently falling rain. Some distance to the right, just visible from where I stood, was the green, placid surface of the pond and the flight of old grey steps leading into it. Ali Khan, our old Moslem bearer, with his wrinkled face and venerable beard, seemed sincerely happy to have me back, and even father displayed unusually high spirits. The eighteen months that followed were the happiest period of my childhood, though even this brief passage of tranquillity was not entirely lacking in intimations of uncertainty.

Whenever I think of home my mind produces a picture, vivid with nostalgic brilliance, of that old silent house standing in its wild, sun-scorched garden. It seems strange to recall that years later, when I lived in the same city, only a few miles from this place of happy memories, I never once took the trouble to visit it. Possibly my failure to do so was based on an instinct of preservation; I knew, perhaps, that it is dangerous to retrace one's footsteps and that the gods have so willed it that none of us can find again that which is lost.

Within a week all kinds of fresh and exciting developments had come my way. Lalsing had taught me to fish in the pond, and I used to sit on a stone step and, mesmerized, watch my small white float bobbing on the green water. I never caught a fish that was more than two inches long, but I had hours of happiness. We acquired a black and white smooth-haired fox terrier named Skip who became my constant companion, and developed the endearing habit of swimming round and round the small pool, creating miniature waves that broke against the grey steps. In place of Sophie, a small, neat, brown-skinned woman appeared, who called herself Mrs Reynolds. She was gentle, addicted to gossip, and used to read to us from an old battered copy of *The Swiss Family Robinson*.

In the stables father's big Waler, which was named, for some inscrutable reason, Angel Face, moved impatiently in his stall, and on one occasion at least, escaped to canter wildly all over the garden, trampling mother's favourite flowers. This happened at night, and eventually father, wearing nothing but the upper portion of his pyjamas and pale with fury, had to rush out to capture him. In a corner of the veranda, leaning against the wall, were father's two guns, a heavy regulation carbine, and a .22 Winchester repeating rifle. I loved the touch and feel of these wonderful, precise instruments of destruction, and this obsession with firearms was to last me for most of my life. It is the fashion now to decry such tastes, but in my case they certainly did not imply the faintest leanings towards murder, but merely an instinctive appreciation of anything skilfully designed to achieve a definite purpose.

Mother, in those early days, must have been an extremely attractive woman. She was tall, nearly five foot nine, in an era when women were generally much shorter, and her graceful neck, beautifully modelled shoulders, and long slim legs might have been designed to make the most of the fashions then in vogue. She had large, clear grey eyes, a short, straight nose, and small, high-arched feet. She radiated tranquillity, and a kind of unchanging faith, and I think that she was as feminine a creature as could be conceived. If this were so, her life with father must, indeed, have offered her meagre comforts, but the strange fact is that she continued to love him to the bitter, sordid end. It may be that her religious beliefs, in addition to simple economic pressures, were partially responsible for this illogical loyalty, but all that I know convinces me that, in spite of everything, she just happened to love one man, and throughout the course of her entire life she chose to give him everything.

Life in that big, old house moved forward with deceptive placidity. Father's star was high and everything he touched achieved dramatic success. He was making considerable sums of money, but not much of his earnings were spent on either the house or his family. He would frequently remain out until the small hours, and at such times mother's anxiety and fear were painful to watch. I can remember her, late at night, pacing the length of the veranda, walking backwards and forwards interminably, dabbing her lips with a small handkerchief, muttering an incoherent confusion of prayers and despair. At such moments she seemed to be almost insane with misgivings and pain. The spec acle of such agony in one who was normally the epitome of tranquillity was terrifying.

At other times father would return to the house bringing half a dozen friends with him, and I knew that these were people whom my mother met with reluctance and distaste. In the noisy chatter that ensued, she would sit, trying to smile, striving to adjust herself to the situation, but I knew that every minute of this apparent conviviality was a bitter and unnecessary ordeal.

Strange men, formal and remote, exuding an oddly bogus optimism and carrying bulging briefcases, appeared frequently and remained alone with father for long hours at a stretch. I learnt that these men were lawyers, and that something sinister referred to as 'our case' was being heard in a vaguely terrifying place known as the High Court. Years had to elapse before a partial understanding of these events became clear to me. I know now that father had left Doyle & Company, after a ferocious quarrel with the chairman, and had started a competitive business on his own. This concern flourished for a while, and then Doyle & Company had instituted proceedings against him, claiming misappropriation of a vast sum of money. The case dragged on for over a year, consuming thousands of rupees in legal expenses. Barristers, solicitors, experts and special witnesses were sucked into the struggle like vultures attracted by the smell of blood. As the months slipped by, the outlook became increasingly dark for father. Powerful forces were arrayed against him, and everyone except himself realized that his cause was almost certainly lost.

But father remained supremely confident, treating his adversaries with disdain. He was certain that the verdict must be in his favour. He refused to listen to the warnings of his friends or to prepare, even at that late stage, for the possibility of defeat. For example, his lawyers suggested that he should put the house and its contents in mother's name, thus ensuring the salvage of some small part of his possessions, in the event of an unfavourable verdict. This he refused to do. With a confidence that seemed close to insanity, and an arrogance that appeared to invite the wrath of the gods, he continued to assert that there was no cause for anxiety. In fact, as the skies collapsed upon him, his mind and body shone with energy and high spirits, almost as though he were revelling in the prospect of destruction.

Although I was increasingly conscious of the shadows that threatened to engulf the family fortunes, I was still young enough to find happiness and wonder all around me. Every morning my brother and I would sit on the sunlit veranda while mother attempted to teach us the rudiments of reading and arithmetic. I failed to shine in these academic experiments. I seemed incapable of adding two and two correctly, and my powers of concentration were far from impressive. Michael easily out-distanced me. Nevertheless, I learnt to read fairly well quite some time before my sixth birthday. Characteristically, I achieved this more or less on my own, simply because I suddenly discovered that I wanted to do so. I can still remember exactly how this happened. I was sitting on the veranda with a large book on my knee, staring intently at a picture which for some reason instantly attracted me. In this picture, a young man, utterly forlorn and dejected, was seen sitting on the floor, his bowed head resting on his arms. A shaft of sunlight slanted down on his despairing figure from a small barred window some distance above his head. The scene contained a mystery, and I was conscious of an urgent need to understand the explanation for his hopeless misery. Word by word I succeeded in reading and partially understanding the print at the bottom page. After that, reading became increasingly easy, and by the time I was seven this was the one subject in which I could easily surpass my brother.

For the rest, I spent hours playing with Skip, or fishing in the still waters of the pond, and every evening the two of us were taken for a long walk by Mrs Reynolds. I recall one incident that left me bitterly disappointed, and acutely conscious of the injustice displayed by the adult world. One afternoon, a bedraggled, almost naked Indian gypsy walked into our compound leading a small brown pony, so thin that its ribs were clearly visible. He offered to sell us this tiny animal for the absurdly small sum of six rupees (about fifty pence) and I was immediately convinced that to possess this creature was all that mattered in my life. I pleaded with my mother to let me have it, but despite all my eloquence she said that she could not do so without first consulting father. The man and the pony settled down to wait for his arrival, while I, throbbing with impatience, remained with the little beast until at last the moment of decision was upon us. Father barely glanced at the pony. 'No,' he said briefly, 'absolutely impossible; we haven't got a spare stable to put it in.' I don't suppose that I was often to plumb the depths of sorrow which I then experienced.

And then, abruptly, terrifyingly, everything began to change and dissolve. Doyle & Company won their case against my father, and consequently he found himself confronted with the prospect of refunding something like £30,000. An appeal was lodged which postponed the agony for several more months, and when this, too, failed, bankruptcy was all that was left. The official receiver took possession of all my father's assets, including the house and all it contained.

And I was to suffer a personal loss which, for me at least, was even more painful than the general collapse. My fox terrier, Skip, was run over late one night by a drunken driver on the road just outside our gate. He was still alive when they carried him into the house, but his lungs had been punctured and he died almost immediately. The sight of this indomitable little animal, once so quick and alert, lying on his side gasping out his life, evoked a horror and a distress that was shared by us all. Father, tense with rage and grief, hurried out to find a vet, but long before his return, with a final, almost apologetic wag of his stumpy tail, Skip, the dauntless swimmer and my inseparable companion, was dead. This disaster left us badly shaken because, in some way, it seemed like an omen sent to prepare us for other even darker misfortunes.

A week later, Angel Face, the big Waler that had been a part of my life for almost as long as I could remember, was led out of his stall for the last time, and that same evening Ali Khan, our patriarchal bearer, who had been with us since my birth, courteously intimated that it was suddenly necessary to return to his ancestral village. Eventually there was no one left except the young Sikh chauffeur who had refused to leave us, though there was now no car for him to drive. Those last few weeks in the old house were filled with gloom and forebodings. Father was in a mood of smouldering fury, convinced that he had been the victim of a cunning and unscrupulous conspiracy. He was incapable of admitting that his own reckless folly was chiefly to blame, nor did he display the slightest awareness of the pain and humiliation borne by my mother.

Her reaction to the collapse of everything that she most valued displayed such dignity and courage that even our worst enemies extended to her the sympathy and admiration she so clearly deserved. Then and later, it was her steadfast loyalty which induced a hostile world to proffer her irresponsible husband the help he so seldom deserved.

After prolonged discussions and frequent changes of plan, it was decided that it would be best for everyone if he was to leave India. He accepted this suggestion with alacrity. 'Australia,' he boomed confidently, striding up and down the veranda. 'That's it; a new country, a new world. Europe is old and tired, and England is too bloody crowded.' But the war was on, and the submarine menace was at its worst. He discovered that months would have to elapse before a passage to Australia would become available. With characteristic impatience, and the kind of irrationality which only he could achieve, he booked a passage to New York, declaring that, once there, it would be easy to find a ship bound for his original choice. Most people might well have concluded that to travel ten thousand miles in the wrong direction was not a particularly satisfactory means to employ to reach somewhere quite different, but he rejected such petty considerations. Within a surprisingly short time, he succeeded in booking our passages on an Ellerman & Hall ship bound for New York via the Cape of Good Hope.

And now, he flung himself into frenzied preparations for this venture. In some fashion which can, perhaps, be left in obscurity, he still possessed the equivalent of two or three thousand pounds, and with this sum, and several enormous wooden packing cases, he was eager to get to sea.

In these circumstances, the entire Greave family, exiled from the sun and rejected by their contemporaries, boarded the *City of Lahore* and set sail for the unknown continent of America.

5

The *City of Lahore* was totally unlike the current conception of a luxury liner. There were no spacious lounges or cocktail bars resplendent in chrome and brilliantly painted murals on her: she was a dour, hardworking cargo ship designed to accommodate a handful of passengers in conditions of spartan simplicity. Every square foot of her, funnel, masts and hull, was painted a dull slate grey, presumably because this depressing shade was considered to make her a less conspicuous target for the German submarines that then infested the oceans. I have only to think of her to smell again the tang of salt air, and the odour of machine oil, fresh paint, and sun-baked steel plates. The second-class passengers, including the Greave family, were accommodated far astern under a narrow deck, cluttered with hatches and ugly black winches stinking of oil and grease. Then came the bleak expanse of an iron well-deck, and beyond that the lofty central structure which included the cabins of the first-class passengers, the funnel and the bridge.

In the months that followed I learnt to know every inch of that ship, from the crew's quarters, far astern, smelling of hot Lascar curries, sweat and stale air, to the extreme tip of the bows, where I could stand beside the great anchor chains and look down and see the sharp prow cutting through the waves like the blade of a giant knife. I was to have ample time for such explorations because, incredible as it may well seem, more than three months had to elapse before the *City of Lahore* finally succeeded in reaching New York. The voyage was prolonged in this way because the ill-fated vessel – possibly the presence of the Greave family represented some kind of jinx – was destined to face almost every known sea disaster. These included death at sea, attempted murder, running aground, and a disastrous fire, not to mention several other minor accidents. I record these facts with some reluctance, realizing that they may sound a shade unlikely, but as they are strictly accurate I have no choice but to set them down.

For many reasons, the memory of that long voyage was to leave indelible marks on my mind. It must be remembered that we were crossing the ocean at a time of war, which meant that we were never free from danger and uncertainty, though I was sufficiently young and resilient to accept these perils with equanimity. When night came, and the second-class passengers sat huddled together in the hot darkness, all of us were conscious of the chill breath of fear. We did not have long to wait for our first disaster. About a week after our departure, one of the passengers, a young American journalist, died of pneumonia. I can still remember the sight of his body, mis-shapen and horrible, encased in a canvas shroud, exposed on the hatch some feet above the deck. Fortunately it was soon concealed under the folds of the American and British flags, and as the passengers stood in a circle, looking lonely and vulnerable under the bright sunlight, surrounded by the immensity of the sea, our captain read the Burial Service. It was all over in a few minutes, and then the flags were removed, and the blurred corpse, mummified in its canvas wrappings, was placed on a sloping plank, down which it slid into the vast depths of the ocean.

Soon afterwards, just as the light was beginning to fade, two sailors, both half-breeds from Brazil, engaged in a savage knife fight on the upper deck. This contest ended when one of the men slumped to the floor, blood pouring from deep wounds in his neck and chest. A few seconds later the victorious assailant, apparently terrified at what he had done, plunged towards the rails, and flung himself overboard. The loud yell of 'man overboard' instantly produced intense excitement and activity.

Passengers hurried to the rails exchanging confused questions and answers, a stentorian shout summoned the boat crews to their quarters. The engine room telegraph jangled from the bridge, as the *City of Lahore* decreased speed, and then turned at a sharp angle, to retrace its course astern. Two boats were lowered, and as their crews scrambled to clear their oars and cut away, the passengers watched the scene, laughing and animated, only partially able to accept the tragic reality of the situation. I missed the initial stages of this drama, because I was curled up in my bunk, fast asleep, for several minutes after the confusion started, When I reached the deck, the night was very dark, and the ship had come to a halt, rolling heavily as it was buffeted by huge, smooth rollers, their peaks glistening with phosphorescent light. About a hundred yards astern, I could see the two boats rising and falling as they fought their way through the heavy swell. I could see the blades of their oars flashing for a second as they bit into the waves and hear the sound of muted voices calling in the darkness. My father explained what had happened in a few terse sentences, and for the next half-hour I stood with the others, watching the boats continue their futile search. And then, suddenly, the tension slackened. Someone said 'It's a waste of time. The screws must have chopped him to bits,' and soon afterwards the boats were hoisted aboard, the engines throbbed, and the *City of Lahore* was once more in motion, pushing rapidly through the night, almost as though it was glad to dissociate itself from a sordid incident.

But events like these were forgotten surprisingly soon. Within a matter of hours the passengers were absorbed again in the trivialities of life at sea. In less than a week the stabbed sailor was seen wandering about the deck, shoulders and arms swathed in bandages, his face thin and haunted, and that was the end of the enigmatic affair. I was certainly not excessively concerned by either of these events. As the ship ploughed doggedly forward, first through the Bay of Bengal, then the Indian Ocean, and approached the Atlantic, a succession of sun-scorched days and starlit nights offered me innumerable adventures and pleasures. I roamed all over the ship, frequently arousing the rage of the officers and deckhands.

In the meantime, my father, with characteristic drive and

confidence, had become a prominent if not a particularly loved member of the small group of second-class passengers. Three or four of these were American missionaries returning to the States with their families. These evangelical types were held in special detestation by my father, and his feelings were certainly reciprocated, though perhaps less openly expressed, by the people involved. But others, including a young theatrical couple, a boisterous Scot named Mackenzie, and a middle-aged writer who specialized in the production of travel books describing outlandish parts of the Far East, were much more to his taste. With them, and others of a similar bent, he proceeded to enliven the tedium of a long voyage. He staged a mock trial in which he, rather inappropriately, chose to play the part of prosecuting counsel, and organized a daily sweepstake, in addition to recurring sessions of community singing. These entertainments were not always a complete success. For example, during the course of the trial, he became so passionately involved with his role as prosecuting counsel that his cross-examination of the various supposed witnesses produced an intensity of emotion that almost led to physical violence between several of the male participants. The sweepstakes, too, caused considerable bickering. But the nightly sing-songs were more successful, and as father possessed a passable baritone, he was frequently requested to sing, which gratified him exceedingly.

He also participated in other activities of a much less sentimental kind. Very soon he had succeeded in quarrelling ferociously with the captain, the first engineer, and most of the missionaries aboard. Very little that he saw on board the ship met with his approval. He criticized the food, the inefficiency of the officer on watch, and the habits of many of his fellow passengers. He was assertive, argumentative and dictatorial, reserving his worst insults for the Americans on board. His recent humiliations in India had apparently left no scars, and he clearly assumed that he was doing the United States a considerable favour by honouring it with his presence.

Then came the next example of the ship's extraordinary capacity for meeting trouble. Between 2.30 and 3 a.m., when everyone except the watch on deck was peacefully sleeping, the *City of Lahore* managed to find a reef and plunge straight on to it. There was a crash, and the sound of steel plates grinding and crumpling as a long strip of steel was torn out of her bottom. Most of the passengers only realized what had happened on the following day, and no one, then or later, seemed to explain this error in navigation. All this happened within fifty miles of Durban, and when we docked it was discovered that the accident was serious enough to require prolonged repairs in dry dock. As it was impossible for us to remain on board in these circumstances, the company arranged for the passengers to be transferred to a hotel, where we remained for the next three weeks.

My memories of Durban are vague, but I do recall that the hotel faced a beautiful golden beach that appeared to extend to the limits of the horizon. I spent scores of happy hours playing on these sands, watching the enormous blue foam-crested waves rushing towards me under the high arc of the sunlit skies. The Durban I remember was full of Indians. Apart from a few rather tatty Zulus, wearing feathers and beads, who dragged rickshaws round for the convenience of the tourists, I cannot recollect confronting a single real African. The hotel staff, the proprietors of the various shops, and the clerks and petty officials were all Indians. It was difficult at times to realize that we were no longer in India, though my father asserted that the Durban Indians were much less docile than their Indian counterparts. But the smell of Africa had a special quality that was instantly recognizable. It was charged with a strange, exuberant vitality, the sign of immense, invisible strength. The smell of India was special, too, but it was redolent of a quality that was somehow tired and exhausted.

I never seemed to get far away from the sea in Durban. I recall walking one night through the docks, and listening to the lisp of the dark tide slipping towards us under the pier. Eventually our ship was refloated, and the passengers, rather reluctantly I think, returned aboard, and we were again under way.

Several days later we reached Cape Town, and entered its beautiful harbour, dominated by Table Mountain. In Cape Town, we met my uncle (strictly my mother's brother-in-law), his wife Mary, and their son 'Minty', who was about my age. My uncle was a bullying, forceful character, a corpulent Scot with a bristling ginger moustache, and I liked neither him nor his spoilt, mischievous son. Cape Town was crowded and prosperous, totally unlike Durban, and I was sorry to leave it after a stay of only three days. But such regrets – though naturally I could not have then guessed it – were unnecessary.

On our first night at sea, again sometime around 3 a.m., the *City of Lahore*, still pursuing its insatiable need for self-destruction, caught fire. On this occasion no one was able to remain asleep during the course of the disaster. Our first intimation that something was wrong was a discreet knock on the cabin door. The knocking continued, and when at last we were all awake, the door opened to disclose the figure of one of the ship's officers standing on the threshold. His expression was composed, but slightly embarrassed, as he said quietly, 'I think you had better get the children dressed, and bring them on deck.' He hesitated, then added primly, 'I am afraid we have run into a little trouble.'

'Trouble? What trouble?' asked my father irritably.

The officer replied reluctantly, 'Well, as a matter of fact, the ship is on fire.'

The next five minutes were animated. My father, cursing 'My God, what will they do next; what a bunch of bloody incompetents', dragged himself out of his bunk and started to get himself out of his pyjamas. My mother, cool but fatalistic, pulled my brother and me out of the warm bedclothes and got to work to clothe us in the kind of attire that might be considered suitable for a prolonged ocean voyage in an open boat. I remember that she forced me to get inside three separate pairs of warm underpants, which gave me a deceptive appearance of corpulence, and when at last she had bundled us into every conceivable kind of warm garment, the Greave family hurried on deck.

Here, the scene presented all the dramatic elements of the traditional disaster at sea. The night was intensely dark, with a heavy dangerous swell rolling the ship from side to side, as it floated with its engines cut. Clouds of thick smoke poured out of the forward hatch, and all round it men were hurrying and shouting as they attempted to aim half a dozen hoses at the invisible fire. The passengers scrambled about in confusion and dismay. The vast majority of them were silent, but some of the missionaries had started to sing hymns, and one of them, an old party with a loud, rich voice, was on his knees, arms outstretched, intoning passionate prayers for our succour. I think that I was too interested to be really scared, but as events progressed I did become conscious of an indefinable, increasing fear.

Everything was in a state of utter confusion; the captain bawling what seemed to be a whole series of contradictory orders from the bridge, while the deck officers leapt about, striving to persuade the passengers to get into their life-jackets and station themselves close to their respective boats. My father, with his gift for stating the obvious, said loudly, 'You're not going to get me into any of those bloody boats. Everyone knows they leak like a sieve,' and as he continued in this optimistic strain, one or two women began to weep mournfully, adding their complaints to his. While all this was going on, the Lascar firemen, shivering in their thin dungarees, became increasingly excited, and shouting at each other in their native tongue, began to press forward in the direction of the boats, with the obvious intention of getting aboard without further delay. Brandishing an enormous revolver, like a villain in a Western movie, the Fourth Officer motioned them back with a great display of fury, while we innocent passengers shrank away from his menacing pistol, which seemed far more likely to destroy one of us than the rebellious Lascars.

Suddenly the figure of the captain emerged through the gloom, and at the appearance of this symbol of ultimate authority, the Lascars retreated and everyone became silent. The captain was a small, lean man, in his early fifties. His long, dispirited face seldom displayed emotion, and his eyes gazed at life with an expression of barely concealed distrust. Now, he looked haggard but composed, and when he spoke his few grudging sentences instantly won awed attention. We learnt that there was no cause for unreasoning panic. The fire continued to burn, but as we were only 120 miles from Cape Town, we would now attempt to return there as soon as possible. He concluded this brief speech by saying sternly, 'I want all passengers to keep their life-jackets on, and remain on deck.' He faced us impassively for a long moment, then turned and made a dignified exit in the direction of the bridge. There was a confused babble of voices as the tension relaxed. I, and several other children, spent what was left of the night sleeping uncomfortably on one of the hard leather seats in the lounge.

The next morning was chill and grey, with a tearing wind, and a rough sea. The *City of Lahore*, rolling heavily, vast clouds of smoke still billowing from the invisible fire, was racing to safety as fast as her engines could carry her. Around 10 a.m. a large ocean-going tug was seen in the distance, heading towards us. We heard later that this vessel had picked up one of our distress signals, and for the rest of that day until the late evening it stuck close beside us. We were back in Cape Town early that night, and now, for the second time, the passengers trooped down the gang-plank, and headed for the nearest hotel. Again our battered ship was out of commission, and once more we were forced to remain on shore until the ravages of the fire had, apparently, been repaired. We were to stay in Cape Town for nearly five weeks, spending most of this time in my uncle's house close to the centre of the city.

It was a relief to be at sea again, because, despite everything, the ship had become like a home to me. On we went, steaming further and further across the Atlantic. Each morning I awoke to see nothing except the vast, lonely face of the ocean. The world of men had vanished, and the only reality was a small grey ship, the hot sunshine, and the huge dome of a cloudless sky. The sea then, and for the rest of my life, exerted a fascination from which I was never to escape. Because it was savage, incalculable and beautiful, I both feared and loved it with a passion which was almost sexual. I was never happier than when close to boats and the sea, and much of my youth was spent close to the ocean. I am sure that the months spent on the *City of Lahore* were greatly responsible for this passion. For me, beauty and fear were inexorably joined, and my early devotion to the sea was a response to various enigmatic tendencies within myself.

We were now in particularly dangerous waters, because here the submarines were said to reap a rich harvest. Precautions were redoubled, and a seaman was posted in the crow's nest a hundred feet above the deck, to watch for anything that resembled a periscope. Late one night we approached land for the last time before the end of the voyage. A dim island emerged from the dark, and the hot, sweet smell of rich earth and tropical flowers drifted across our decks. No one was allowed to land. The ship anchored in the beautiful but dangerous harbour, and lighters loaded with coal came alongside. The coaling was done by hand, a long line of ragged, singing Negroes, each burdened with a heavy sack, hurrying along a narrow plank. Finally we were at sea again, and now, as the air became colder and the sunshine less strong, we knew that our journey was drawing to an end.

So, after a voyage that had lasted nearly four months, the *City of Lahore* approached the towering skyline of New York. It was a clear, bright evening with the wind driving small, puffy clouds across a blue sky. We breathed a new air, filled with vitality and strength. The harbour was crowded with shipping, and as the famous skyline loomed ever nearer, the American passengers lined the rails, drinking in the sight of home. As they expressed their admiration, my father, watching the scene with sombre distaste, murmured 'I don't think much of it. And what's that damn fool statue doing stuck out in the middle of nowhere?' But no one listened to these grudging remarks. The long voyage was over, and even then each one of us was preparing himself for a new and different life.

6

The New York I recall is not very like the gigantic, savage, almost paranoic city that now bears that name. I remember the era of the T Model Ford; the Stutz Racer; the one cent lollipop; the dime stores; milk wagons drawn by big, patient horses, that were transformed into sleighs for the coming of winter; the *Saturday Evening Post*; and the movies, still soundless, showing *The Four Horsemen of the Apocalypse* for only 15 cents. It was the time of Jack Dempsey; the death of Caruso – 'They wanted a songbird in Heaven, so God took Caruso there'; Babe Ruth; Barnum and Bailey; the Shimmy and Al Jolson. It was, in fact, the threshold of the roaring twenties when the USA, throbbing with energy and confidence, was the richest, strongest country in the world.

My very first impression of America has an unreal, dreamlike quality. It is dark, and my mother, my brother and I are seated on a vast wharf, staring into the sullen waters of the harbour. Some distance to the right, the stern of the *City of Lahore*, now deserted, looms above us like a wall. All the other passengers have disembarked, but we have been left waiting for the return of my father, who has been arguing with the customs authorities for several hours. Those wretched, mysterious packing cases which he had insisted on bringing with him had produced unexpected and prolonged hostility from the port officials. Isolated on that shadowy pier, we were all approaching the ultimate in boredom and fatigue.

Eventually, soon after midnight, when both my brother and I were so sleepy that we could no longer sit upright, my father summoned a taxi and bundled us into the rear seat, where we immediately lost consciousness. In this blissful state, temporarily deserted by our parents, and alone in an unknown city, we were driven to the Hotel Begorian, which had presumably been contacted by my father some time earlier. When we got there – though I was only to hear this on the following morning – a kindly Italian maid, big-boned and elderly, carried us both, still sleeping, inside the hotel, and finally deposited us in an enormous, old-fashioned bed.

When we awoke the next morning to the smell of fresh rolls and good American coffee, the sun was shining, and my father and mother were with us. We were on the thirteenth floor, and as we looked down into the crowded street, throbbing with life and movement, I think we were all conscious of a mood of excited anticipation. This was America, the new, rich world, and the keen air had a quality that was like a challenge. A mood of unusual happiness and confidence took possession of us all. Lunch was brought in by the same helpful maid, and for the next few hours we were all busily engaged in unpacking suitcases and trunks. Soon afterwards we were out in the streets, a part of the swarming millions that hurried endlessly between the towering skyscrapers. We got a taxi, and drove through Times Square, Columbus Circle, and the opulent length of Fifth

Avenue. The war was nearly over, and the atmosphere of the city was an almost hysterical blend of high spirits and relief.

We remained at the Hotel Begorian for something like six weeks. After the first couple of days, we saw little of my father, who was out until late at night, presumably informing the great commercial organizations of the city that he was there to offer them the use of his vast acumen and experience. During the hours when we were alone, my mother read or talked to us, and with the passage of time we became increasingly friendly with one or two members of the staff. Our new life was completely different from anything we had known before, but as far as I can remember, neither my brother nor myself experienced the least difficulty in adjusting to it. At the age of seven I seem to have discovered that change and uncertainty were a part of my destiny. I liked most Americans, while paying lip service to my father's unchanging and fiery denunciations of almost everything that the USA had to offer.

And then, miraculously, unbelievably, the war was over, and New York went mad on the day that the Armistice was signed. There was a parade down Broadway. The doughboys were home again or at least there were an astonishing number of them knocking around who had apparently never left home. Anyway, the soldiers marched, the bands played, and New York gave them its traditional ticker-tape welcome. There were flags everywhere, every shop and individual displayed the star-spangled banner, and amongst these huge, boisterous crowds, my brother and I, patriots to the last, marched about waving two diminutive Union Jacks.

My father made it clear that he was not engaged in anything as commonplace as searching for a job, but was rather examining the merits of a dozen brilliant openings to decide which one of them should be honoured by his presence. He had forgotten his earlier ambition of reaching Australia, and was now reconciled to remaining in the new world. 'I think I can show these Yankees a thing or two about running a business,' he asserted confidently, and sure enough, in less than a month he actually found a post with Duncan Brothers, a long-established English business operating in New York. He was placed in charge of a department and received a salary of five hundred dollars a month, plus a commission of ten per cent on all deals which he initiated. Most men would have accepted this as a stroke of almost incredible good luck, but my father displayed neither gratitude nor surprise.

I believe we left the Hotel Begorian sometime late in 1918, and moved to a small white house in Yonkers. Our new address (it seems extraordinary that I can still remember it after a gap of over fifty years) was 45 Livingstone Avenue, and our new home, prim and antiseptic, was one of a long line of similar houses. We had now become a part of middle-class suburbia, and I am sure that none of our genteel, hard-working neighbours then realized the lawless eccentricity of the strangers in their midst. But for the first few months everything went smoothly enough. Very unwisely, as I now think, my mother arranged for the two of us to attend a nearby Catholic school known as St Peter's. This school was certainly an extremely unsatisfactory choice, as its pupils were drawn from the less savoury elements of the Irish and Italian communities. It was disorganized and rowdy, and the boys, authentic roughnecks from the side-walks of New York, seemed to spend most of their energy in a series of bloodthirsty fights. To these young tearaways, my brother and I were as alien as creatures from a different planet. Our accents, for example, instantly produced a communal reaction of astonished horror. During the first weeks we had only to open our lips to be surrounded by a mob of startled young Americans. 'Dese guys sure do speak English kinda funny. For Christ's sake, why don't you learn to speak real American?' This was the general opinion, expressed in the rich dialect of the Micks and Wops.

Yet after a comparatively short time I was accepted as a somewhat unusual but not unlikeable member of the gang. Judged by British standards, the kids were warm-hearted and demonstrative, and I soon found a special and loyal friend in a young Irishman, a year or two older than myself, named Kelly. This boy possessed a particularly rebellious, reckless temperament, and as he was generally accepted as a leader by the rest, his support undoubtedly saved me from many perils. He was an odd, likeable character but such was his instinctive distaste for any kind of authority that I feel sure he must have eventually accepted the hospitality of one or other of the state prisons. For some reason he liked me very much, but only so long as it was clearly understood that he was the boss. He had the endearing habit of slipping his arm round my shoulder, pulling me towards him, and saying almost coaxingly, 'Can I lick you, Pete?' This question left me somewhat embarrassed; but always inclined towards peace, and unwilling to offend him, I would mumble vaguely, 'Yes, yes, sure, anything you say,' at which he would smile with unrestrained happiness, and our alliance went on without a discordant note.

Then, one unhappy morning, more by chance than anything else, we actually started to fight, and to my utter astonishment it soon became clear that I was punching a little harder and faster than my old ally. The fight was never finished, but from that moment young Kelly never spoke to me again. His temperament was such that any sort of equal relationship was impossible for him to accept. I still remember his loss with a pang of real sadness.

One afternoon some months after we had joined the school, some of the older boys, louts of sixteen and seventeen, surrounded me as I was returning home. I don't think they meant me any particular harm, but were simply intrigued by what seemed to them my extraordinary accent. Suddenly one of them, perhaps attacked by momentary boredom, gave me a violent push, and I fell forward striking my face against a small thorny bush. When I rose my right eye was streaming with blood, and at this evidence of their handiwork, my assailants rapidly withdrew, leaving me to stumble sadly towards Livingstone Avenue. When I reached there, my eye was still bleeding, and the doctor when he arrived, said that I was lucky not to have lost my sight. This unfortunate incident persuaded my mother to withdraw us both from the crude but exciting atmosphere of this, my first American school.

Early in December the snow came. Cars lurched down the frozen streets, their tyres festooned with steel skid chains; the big horse-drawn milk wagons discarded their wheels and glided along on long metal runners; pedestrians plodded forward wearing ghastly rubber over-shoes known as galoshes. Livingstone Avenue sprouted several small, mis-shapen snowmen, while soggy snowballs curved through the air. A huge, stout, coloured woman named Ellen, who hailed from Georgia and spoke with a Southern accent as rich as molasses, took over our kitchen, and we adopted a tiny, white kitten. And then, when Christmas was upon us, mother suddenly vanished, and my father's replies to our anxious enquiries seemed oddly vague and unsatisfactory. It appeared from what he said that she had gone into some mysterious hospital to produce what he called a little baby, but he proffered this explanation with such guilt and reluctance, that I could only conclude that he was lying. He became abnormally kind, visiting us every morning while we were still in bed and leaving packets of candy on our table. But just about the time when I had more or less made up my mind that he had probably done her in, a taxi appeared and took us all to the hospital.

Surprisingly enough she was still alive, though lying in bed, blanketed to the chin. She was holding something in her arms that was pink and pulpy, and seemed vaguely alive. Everyone smiled and looked at me, apparently expecting evidence of intense gratification, but I was unable to show much enthusiasm. When asked what I thought of my new little sister, I reflected for a moment, and then replied that she reminded me of a mustard plaster. This remark was not particularly well received, and we drove home in slightly embarrassed silence. A few days later, mother returned, but it was some time before we were able to adjust ourselves to the presence of this queer pink bundle, who either howled, or sucked at parts of my mother that were generally concealed. She was named Mary, and almost immediately demonstrated a restless, energetic disposition.

I cannot now remember the exact time when I first became fully aware of the addiction which was responsible for ruining not only my father's life but also the fortunes of all of us. I am sure that this must have occurred at some point during our first two years in New York, and I am equally convinced that it was unlikely to have happened in a matter of seconds, the result of a single lightning flash of revelation. In all probability the process was slow and cumulative, the product of a hundred fragments of partially understood conversations and gossip which led to a moment when further doubt was impossible. When at last our eyes were opened we were confronted by a situation which was not only tragic, but slightly ridiculous.

It appeared that our father was an exhibitionist, and that this grotesque appetite drove him forward with persistent, unchanging force. I remember my mother telling us years later that soon after their marriage she was pleased and flattered by his repeated requests to her to play the piano. Every evening, soon after he returned from work, he would say coaxingly, 'Play something for me; I love to listen to your music.' My mother, in her simplicity, would obediently sit at the piano, open the music, and play for an hour and a half, or even longer. Whenever she paused or hesitated, she would hear his voice, enjoining her to fresh efforts. 'Go on, don't stop,' he would say persuasively, and thus encouraged, my mother would continue to play. She was to learn in due course that while she was engrossed in striking the keys, her husband had stationed himself on the veranda, completely absorbed in exposing himself to a woman in the adjacent house. He was, of course, totally indifferent to Bach or Beethoven; they were only important because my mother's attention was temporarily distracted from him. She was to learn that in order to satisfy the needs of this idiotic compulsion, he was capable of extravagant lying, and an ingenuity in deception which was beyond belief. He would practise his obsession every day; sometimes several times a day, and at the most unlikely times and places. Generally he succeeded in getting away before the alarm was raised, but necessarily there were occasions when he was not so lucky. This macabre hobby must have brought him close to death on hundreds of occasions; husbands threatened him with revolvers; mobs pursued him through the darkness of bazaars; he was abused by indignant women, and escaped by a hair's breadth from the forces of the law.

Had he been mentally unstable, this inexplicable addiction would at least have evoked a certain sympathy, and might have been left to medical care and supervision. But, apart from this fatal indiosyncrasy, he was not only completely sane but also extremely intelligent and enterprising. Psychiatrists spent hundreds of hours delving into the labyrinths of his unconscious, but in the end none of them was prepared to assert that he was not fully responsible for his actions, nor could they discover a way of curing his mysterious affliction. Its destructive force was destined to poison and destroy his entire life. When he was not actively engaged in the performance of this bizarre activity, he was thinking about it, and when he was not thinking about it, the consequences of his excesses left him little time for anything else. It was impossible for him to have a friend, because the intimacy inseparable from such a relationship represented a restraint which he found impossible to accept. His strong, forceful personality attracted friends, but their presence soon bored and irritated him and the association would end in a furious, unnecessary quarrel. This characteristic also ensured that my mother found it impossible to establish any kind of permanent relationship. If she brought women friends to the house, it was necessary for her to remain constantly on the scene, because immediately she was out of sight he was sure to enliven the proceedings by his usual ghastly performance. My mother would return to find the woman rigid with indignation and astonishment, while my father confronted her with an expression of exaggerated innocence. In this, and a hundred other ways, this wretched addiction hung like a cloud, not only over him but over everyone with whom he came in contact.

It may sound incredible, but I am fairly sure it was almost never openly discussed between my father and mother. There was, though, one occasion on which I know that my mother poured out the rage and humiliation that she had so long kept concealed. Dusk had fallen, and they were seated side by side on the small veranda at the back of the house. I can only presume that the evidence of some particularly unpleasant episode had come to light, because my mother, torn with shame and fury, released the agony of years in a bitter onslaught. My father listened to her, silent and motionless, until at last my mother lost the last vestige of control. She raised her hand, and struck him with all her strength across the face, and at this he bowed his head and murmured indistinctly a single sentence: 'I can't help it.' These four words expressed such an extremity of helpless despair that my mother's fury was instantly replaced by a reaction of intense love and compassion, and I do not think that she ever again voluntarily discussed this dark secret. It was accepted as a malignant element which could be neither changed nor questioned, though its shadow hung over the rest of our lives. Because of it we lived like nomads, moving from place to place, pursued by increasing insecurity and poverty.

I recall my mother relating yet another incident. The two of them were travelling by train across the wastes of Russia. Early one morning the train stopped at a small station. After a few minutes my father, still attired in pyjamas and a dressing gown, rose suddenly to his feet, explaining that he wanted to stretch his legs on the crowded platform. In another second, he had disappeared into the unfamiliar landscape. As time passed, and he did not reappear, my mother's anxiety became increasingly difficult to control. Eventually a gong sounded, and with a loud hissing of steam, the train started to move. And then, at the very last moment, he emerged, running towards the rapidly disappearing coach, climbing aboard in the nick of time. His flushed face, heavy breathing, and disordered clothes left no room for doubt in my mother's mind. I only mention this relatively insignificant episode because it underlines the fact that he was capable of involving himself in trouble at the most unlikely times and places.

Yet my father was so much more than the total of his ridiculous obsession. I remember him still with a combination of love and awe. I always longed with passionate intensity for his approbation, and it is sad to record that I was seldom successful in winning it. His courage and vitality, the impact of his unconquerable, soaring spirit, was the more impressive because of the monstrous flaw from which he could never escape. Like a figure in a Greek tragedy, doomed by the will of the gods, he followed his desperate way with a zest and energy that nothing could diminish.

My father complained that Duncan Brothers were unbelievably slow and unenterprising and he was constantly pressing them to allow him to experiment with new ventures. At last he discovered what he believed to be the perfect answer to his problem. A new car, colourfully named the Dixie Flyer, had been presented to the American public. Where or how it was made I shall never know, nor what caused its swift and total obliteration, but it was perhaps inevitable that my father and this short-lived, exotic creation should come together. He interviewed the manufacturers and was offered the sole rights for distributing these cars on the overseas market. There are probably not more than half a dozen people now alive who even remember the Dixie Flyer's brief bid for glory, but for many reasons I am never likely to forget it.

Seething with impatience, and absolutely convinced that he had discovered a second Eldorado, my father lost no time in presenting the results of these negotiations to his elderly, cautious board of directors. Persuasive and eloquent, he painted a wonderful picture of the magnificent possibilities such a venture was sure to produce. He insisted that South Africa was metaphorically starving for just such a car as the Dixie Flyer, and that he was certain to sell hundreds, if not thousands of these vehicles within a very few months, His directors, patient, kindly men, with no desire at all to venture into the uncertainties of such an enterprise, listened to his proposals with barely concealed distrust. But in the end, battered, and partially stupefied by his stubborn persistence, they agreed to let him go. They consented to pay his expenses for an exploratory visit to South Africa which, under no circumstances, was to last more than six months. At the end of that time, he must either produce definite proof of a promising and continued market, or return home with the admission that he had been wrong.

In a mood of triumphant exhilaration, he broke the news to mother. He explained that he had arranged for her to receive monthly payments of three hundred dollars during his absence, adding that although this sum was insufficient to pay for the house, he had temporarily booked cheaper accommodation on South Broadway. 'I'll only be away for six months,' he assured her optimistically, 'and once I get back we'll have enough money to find ourselves something much better than this.' Mother listened to him in silence. She had already learnt the futility of opposing him in such circumstances. Within a week, he and his luggage disappeared in a taxi bound for the docks, and she was left to fend for herself.

Our new home was a five-roomed apartment on the fourth floor of a rather seedy block of flats on South Broadway. It represented a definite descent in the social scale, as this section of the city was neither as quiet nor as select as the area we had just vacated. Trams jangled on the street below us, which was crowded right through the day with a great mass of traffic speeding to and from central New York. But if the street in front of us was noisy and congested, there was a large empty space, overgrown with bushes and grass behind us. Our neighbours here were much less genteel than the prim residents of Livingstone Avenue; they were real New Yorkers, which meant that they belonged to pretty well every known portion of Europe and the Near East. We were surrounded by Irish, Italians, Jews, Armenians and the products of a dozen other races. It must have been extremely difficult for mother to adjust herself to this new, garish environment, but this is exactly what she succeeded in doing.

Ellen, our coloured help, had disappeared, and in her place came Anna, a muscular young Austrian, as strong as a man, solid and thick-waisted, who could only speak rudimentary English. She cooked, swept and laundered with indomitable energy, and soon became mother's staunch ally and friend. The flat was not very large, and with Mary, now seven months old, crawling with extraordinary speed from room to room, and the disorder which my brother and I always left behind us, there never seemed enough room for all of us.

This was the time when I learnt a little about fighting and a lot about running. This knowledge was forced upon me because South Broadway and its surroundings were infested with roving gangs of young Italians, Negroes and Irish, all engaged in continuous warfare. I soon learnt that I had only to step outside the safety of our front door to enter a region where the law of the jungle prevailed. In this bloodthirsty territory a boy could only survive by fighting or running, or joining some clan large and strong enough to offer him protection. Because we had refused to ally ourselves to any of these groups, we had only to venture into the street to be attacked by whatever marauders first happened to sight us. A loud howl, the swift clatter of feet, and our assailants would be upon us. 'We're going to kick the living shit out of you limey bastards,' or 'Wanna fight?' were the usual openings, and after that it was simply a question of slugging it out, or racing for safety. I never enjoyed fighting; I suppose I must have lacked the killer instinct, but as I was tall and strong for my age, and possessed remarkably good reflexes, I often managed to acquit myself quite creditably. I reckon that in that first year, I must have exchanged punches with thirty or forty different opponents. Naturally the vast majority of these scraps only lasted a few seconds, and I hope it will not seem like boasting if I say that, when matched with anyone of approximately my own size, I was seldom beaten.

It may sound illogical, but I am sure that a great part of this success was due to the fact that I was a perfect, de luxe example of a coward. I fought well because I was too scared to do anything else. When fists were flying and there was the smell of blood and sweat in the air, pure funk filled my veins with so much excess adrenalin that I was temporarily possessed with fantastic strength and determination.

We were constantly harassed by an Italian boy named Felix, stocky and vociferous, who was slightly older and larger than myself. This youth, because of his prowess as a fighter and strategist, was the leader of a sizeable Italian gang, and because he lived in the same block of flats as ourselves, was in a particularly advantageous position to spring on us at the most unlikely moments. His father, a tall, scruffy man, was supposed to be the janitor in charge of the building in which we lived. He occupied the basement, and I would often see him, unshaven and partially drunk, wandering about the grounds, sullen and suspicious, searching, apparently for some object on which to vent his wrath. By now Prohibition, and all the complications it entailed, had become a part of American life, and it was rumoured that he operated a small still for the production of illicit alcohol in the privacy of his grimy quarters.

Although unprepossessing, Mr Bartelloni as he was called, seldom troubled us, but this immunity certainly did not apply to his son. He would ignore us for several days, and then suddenly, for no explicable reason, gripped by homicidal fury, he would rush upon us, gesticulating wildly, shouting threats and abuse, compelling us to scatter like leaves pursued by a high wind. In our youthful world, Felix, like some miniature Ghengis Khan, represented the ultimate in terror and uncertainty. Eventually the moment came when, most unwillingly, I found myself forced to challenge his supremacy in single-handed combat, but I shall tell that story later.

If the world outside was often filled with fear and hostility, my life contained many other things that were much more pleasant. Without the presence of my father, mother seemed to draw increasingly close to us. She would read to us every day, and when not absorbed in a book, we would sit for hours listening to her stories of her father's early life in India.

When she was not reading, I can still see her sitting comfortably in her big armchair, head bowed over her sewing as she let her mind float backwards through the years. The cold darkness outside pressed against the windows, and from the street below the muted throb of passing traffic was just audible, but her memory had drifted away from this alien world, and returned to the scorching, Indian sunlight. She spoke quietly, almost indistinctly, not so much talking to us, as retracing the labyrinth of the past for her own pleasure. She must have been very lonely at times, and because we were all she had, she spoke to us exactly as though we were adult.

We had joined another school soon after my father's departure. In contrast to St Peter's, this was rather a refined, bourgeois establishment, run by an order of Roman Catholic nuns. This school, with its spotless classrooms, flowers and decorations, catered for children drawn from a relatively opulent stratum of society, and from the first, both my brother and I felt singularly out of place there. It was a mixed school, and in my class there were several pretty, well-dressed girls whose presence influenced me strongly. My boisterous efforts to win their admiration were not particularly successful, although there was an occasion when I was able to persuade one of them to return home with me. The boys, after the roughnecks I had encountered at St Peter's, struck me as fairly contemptible, and I was pretty sure that I could have licked any two of them with one hand tied behind my back.

The morning's work would start with what was then known as Palmer's writing, which consisted of making endless spirals in a copy-book, which futile exercise was supposed to teach us 'finger control', and thus develop the flexibility which in due course would be used as the foundation for a legible, flowing script. I sometimes wonder what happened to Mr Palmer and his ingenious plan, because I certainly never met it again in any other school. My brother and I were considered unruly and insolent, and on one occasion, when I called one of the little girls 'an ass', our teacher wrote home to complain that I had made use of an obscene word. Before trooping into class, the children gathered in a small chapel, decorated with statues of the Virgin Mary and various other saints. In this setting we would start the day by singing a hymn, the first few lines of which are still embedded in my memory:

> Guardian Angel ever at my side,
> How loving must thou be,
> To leave thy home in Heaven above,
> To guard a little child like me

This was the time when I first attempted to express an aspect of my personality which was often destined to bring me close to destruction in the years that lay ahead. I refer to my habit – it would perhaps be more accurate to use the word addiction – for falling suddenly and violently in love with women of unpredictable tastes and hearts of pure ice. I started, modestly enough, by lavishing my affection on a doll-faced seven-year-old, with blonde hair and beautiful, calculating blue eyes. I did everything I could to attract this girl's attention, but Rose – how deceptive a name can be – turned away in disdain, however energetically I executed cart-wheels or displayed my prowess by fighting with my companions. It was clear that some other, more compelling form of seduction had to be devised. I gave this problem long and careful consideration, and finally found a possible solution. I remembered that there was a large box of chocolates, still half full in one of my mother's cupboards, and I felt sure that with a little luck I could get hold of this box without being detected. Love had proved a failure, and therefore, there seemed nothing for it but a more mercenary approach.

Anxious to put my fortunes to the test, I waylaid the elusive Rose that same afternoon as she was on the point of leaving school. Placing myself in front of her, I said with all the innocent candour that can only belong to complete inexperience, 'Hello Rose, will you walk home with me?' The little girl looked at me suspiciously. 'No,' she said scornfully, 'I gotta get back to my Mom.' This was the response I had expected, but now, like a gambler risking everything on a single card, I played my ace. 'Ah, come on,' I said temptingly, 'I'll give you lots of chocolates,' and as I spoke I held out my two cupped hands to indicate the quantity I had in mind. Rose appeared to reflect. 'Who wants your chocolates? I've got plenty of candy at home.' But her voice seemed to lack conviction. We looked at each other for a long moment, then, guileful as Machiavelli I said softly, 'They're big cream ones with nuts on top.' She hesitated, then surrendered, and a little while later, I was walking triumphantly beside her down Broadway. I don't think we exchanged a single word, but after a while I slid my hand through her arm, and to my surprise she actually snuggled up close to me.

When we reached home, I left her outside, and rapidly climbed the stairs to our flat. My luck was in, no one was visible in the living-room, and in a matter of seconds, I had opened the cupboard, seized the box, and was hurriedly retracing my steps back to Rose. She was standing exactly where I had left her, glancing uneasily around her, but as I appeared and began scooping the contents of the box into her greedy paws, her face brightened, and she smiled. All would have been well, had not mother, for some inscrutable reason, chosen that exact moment to peer out of the window. She was rewarded by the sight of her son, sixty or seventy feet below her, busily engaged in the task of distributing the family's chocolates to a small girl. Completely engrossed in this spectacle, she silently motioned to my brother to join her, and share her enjoyment of the scene.

I only describe this naive fragment from my childhood, because it reveals something of my reckless disregard for consequences when confronted with the compulsive forces of sex. The trouble then and later was that when, to put it politely, my emotions were involved, I lacked the capacity for patience or restraint. This incident, which, by the way, I was never allowed to forget, convinced mother that her elder son's sexual instincts were not to be trusted, and that, like another unlucky figure, I was prone to love not wisely, but too well.

But life at home was peaceful and secure. The muscular, talkative Anna appeared every morning at 8 o'clock, and like a small explosion, flung herself into the various household chores. She was an immigrant, with a fund of colourful stories covering her early experiences in the USA. Soon after her arrival, incapable of speaking a single word of English, she asked an Austrian friend to teach her the English word for 'Thank you'. He explained that the Americans always expressed gratitude by saying 'Fuck you', and for some days the innocent creature made use of her new-found knowledge, and was utterly bewildered at the expressions of rage which it evoked. A year later, she had married a German taxi-driver, but despite the arrival of two children, this partnership had proved a disappointment. 'All he wanted,' she told my mother, 'was the bedding and the beating,' and it seems that she hardly ever emerged without a black eye and sundry bruises. After three years, he had simply failed to return one night, and was never heard of again.

Sometimes Anna would be accompanied by her two children, and they would spend the day at our flat. When this happened, my brother and I were expected to play with them, but this was not easy, as Anna's progeny, genuine little roughnecks from the East Side, regarded us with barely concealed contempt. By their standards we were 'cissies', a word then used to express the ultimate in weakness and ineptitude. The boy must have been about thirteen, a sullen character entirely lacking the forthright, simple virtues of his mother. The girl was blonde, spoilt, and already, at the age of eleven acutely conscious of sex and all it entailed. Because both these children had been born in the States, they regarded their immigrant mother with something like shame, and openly mocked her broken English and old-world traditions. They would sprawl about the flat, bored and cheeky, until at last the lot of us would be packed off to go to a movie, or on a shopping expedition. The first time we went to the movies, they behaved so badly that, after several warnings, the four of us were ejected by an angry usher. And when we went shopping, I was horrified to observe that the girl practised shoplifting in every store we visited and, even worse, that she performed these thefts with such inefficiency that I expected her to be apprehended at any moment. Anna would spend hours relating her children's numerous misadventures to my mother. The boy had already appeared twice in the juvenile courts, and it appeared that the girl had been discovered naked in the home of a middle-aged man. The gulf that divided them from their mother, brought up as a peasant in some small Austrian village, was enormous, and this divergence of ideals and values represented an aspect of American life that was only too common.

In the meantime, news of my father's adventures in Africa was vague in the extreme. Every month or so, mother would receive a brief note from him, some written in a mood of deep depression, others reporting that he was on the point of achieving commercial victories of immense importance. I forgot to say that when he left for Cape Town, he took with him not only the agency for the Dixie Flyer, but also another agency for what were then known as Aladin Houses. These were small, wooden bungalows, built in separate sections, and their special merit consisted in the fact that it was supposed to be possible to erect them from floor to ceiling in the space of twenty-four hours. My father was convinced that these cleverly devised houses would sell like hot cakes in a rapidly growing country like South Africa, but these hopes were shattered even before the voyage was over. By a stroke of singular bad luck, while his ship was still at sea, the South African Government enacted laws forbidding the erection of wooden houses because of the fire risk involved. This was not a promising omen, but my father, confident of his main weapon, the brilliant Flyer, refused to be dismayed. But apparently, fresh and more complicated difficulties had arisen as soon as he landed. The exact nature of these problems was not easy to understand, but he referred bitterly to a demonstration run which had been tragically cut short by the Dixie Flyer suddenly stopping miles from anywhere. This had not created a favourable impression, and his failure to restart the engine had been even more humiliating. In the end, he and his passenger, who was, of course the most influential car dealer in Cape Town, were forced to trudge a couple of miles under a scorching sun before they reached the nearest garage.

This mishap seemed to have produced both rage and astonishment in my father, but it did not come as a surprise to his family; even I was aware that my father's knowledge of cars consisted solely of his ability to drive them. We gathered that he had decided almost immediately that the South African business community were a particularly stupid lot, prone to unreasonable suspicion and irritating procrastination. He seemed to be travelling extensively, as his letters were written from Johannesburg, Pretoria, Port Elizabeth and New London. And mother also received other, more ominous reports of his exploits from her sister in Cape Town. These letters informed her that father had already succeeded in leaving his mark on Africa. He was certainly not killing himself with hard work, and spent most of his time amusing himself in the company of rather questionable types, including a blonde Afrikaans woman. The final shock was to hear that he had joined a tennis club, which left my mother speechless as she was absolutely certain that her husband knew nothing, and cared less, about the game.

As time passed, he appeared to drift further and further away from South Africa. Sometimes the postmarks on his letters indicated that he was in Tanganyika, then Kenya and finally the Belgian Congo. We were never to learn the full details of all that happened to him during his absence, but it soon became abundantly clear that the unfortunate Dixie Flyer had been discarded for other more colourful interests.

7

As my father wandered through Africa, our life in New York progressed peacefully enough. Mother had an instinctive affection and love for her fellow human beings, and within a surprisingly short time had become friendly with the most unlikely people. The milkman would stand at our doorstep discussing his matrimonial problems for what seemed hours at a stretch; book salesmen would attempt to sell her encyclopedias, and end by telling her their life story. Even the big Irish cop, Michael Sullivan, would leave his beat to tell her hair-raising stories of local hold-ups and gang warfare. She had a gift for listening to people, with a kind of aloof but kindly detachment, which seldom failed to extract confidences from the most unlikely sources.

For my brother and me, Saturday afternoon was the high point of the week. Mary, who had now reached the stage of standing upright and lurching erratically from one piece of furniture to another, was left in the charge of Anna, while the rest of us set off for the movies. These excursions were filled with excitement and adventure. We would board a trolley car, and journey towards Yonkers' main shopping centre. Once there, we would march happily into the Metropolitan Picture Palace, a rather seedy establishment which in those economical days charged exactly fifteen cents for reasonably comfortable seats. And now we were engulfed in an enchanted world, silent except for the feverish melodies extracted from a single piano, and for the next three hours life would achieve a magic that left reality far behind.

Apart from my brother, I had two real friends. The first was a small, thin boy with a long pale face and a thatch of stringy blond hair named Emerson Nine. He was a recent arrival to New York, and hailed from California, where his mother had been employed by the Metro-Goldwyn studios as an 'extra'. His father seemed to have disappeared at some point in the distant past and as his mother was out for long periods, presumably working in the city, her son was often alone for hours at a stretch. My other friend was a Canadian, Jack Kavan, strong and dogged, but unfortunately his mind worked so slowly that he might easily have been mistaken for a case of retarded development. These boys were my inseparable companions; we formed a microscopic gang, brought together by our mutual fear of those other, more powerful groups which looked upon us as their legitimate prey.

Late one morning young Emerson appeared, looking very much the worse for wear. He sported a magnificent black eye, and there was an ugly bruise close to his mouth. His explanation, interrupted by loud sniffles, was terse and only too easy to believe. It seems that he had been sent shopping on the previous evening, and when he emerged from the store, both arms laden with a large box containing a dozen eggs, butter, and various other groceries, he was horrified to find himself confronted by the ruthless Felix, accompanied by two of his henchmen. Felix reacted with characteristic fury and speed. Saying briefly, 'Leave this guy to me,' he stepped forward and faced his victim, who could neither run nor attempt to fight. Smiling happily, Felix first measured the distance between them, and then, drawing back his right fist, carefully drew a bead on his target. A fraction of a second later,

BANG, his large, hard fist struck Emerson's face, and the process was repeated several times.

We sat discussing this outrage for some time. Each one of us vied with the other in describing the vengeance we should have liked to inflict on this tyrannical, insolent enemy. And then, carried by the force of my own eloquence, I suddenly realized that I had talked myself into a position from which I could not retreat. I cannot now remember exactly what I said, but I am absolutely certain that all I intended to convey was that I was personally not in the least scared of Felix, and that in the event of various unspecified contingencies, I would be prepared to take him on. The point is that I had no intention of offering to fight him there and then, but rather to state that as a general principle I was not unwilling to consider such a possibility at some nameless date. However not for the first time, my unfortunate fluency had led me on.

My first intimation that something was wrong occurred so quickly that for a time I was left completely speechless. Emerson Nine hurried forward, seized my hand, and shook it vigorously. Jack Kavan, smiling broadly, thumped me on the back, and even my brother's normal expression of aloof detachment changed to a smirk of approval. Praise and encouragement descended on me like a deluge, voices choked with emotion vying to extol my decision. This flood of admiration was pleasant enough, but even then it occurred to me, that all this adulation would be of very little practical use, while I was in the process of being cut to ribbons by the infuriated Felix. I lifted my head, and opened my mouth to utter the words that would instantly have dispelled their dreams, but when I saw their faces, I realized that I had already gone too far to draw back.

I happened to know that Felix would not be available until late evening, as he had been taken into the city for an appointment with the dentist and a later interview with the parole officer. This meant that I could count on five or six hours of blissful immunity, and always an optimist, I tried to believe that something could still occur to prevent his return. 'Perhaps he'll die under the gas,' I told myself hopefully, 'or maybe the parole officer will decide to pack him off to reform school once and for all.' Temporarily reassured by these insubstantial hopes, I did my best to forget the menacing future, and make the most of my brief period of glory. I was not accustomed to the role of hero, and I must admit that I found it extremely enjoyable. Emerson Nine said anxiously, 'You're looking a bit pale. For heaven's sake, relax, and take it easy.' They decided that I was probably hungry, and in need of extra vitamins, and Kavan instantly hurried away, to return laden with ice cream cones, bars of chocolate, and various other sweets. They fed me with almost maternal solicitude, and hung on every word I let fall as though they were listening to an oracle.

And then, Emerson Nine suddenly decided that what I needed was exercise. 'You've got to be toughened up,' he said enthusiastically, and despite my vague protests this suggestion instantly met with general approval.

For the next hour and a half, the three of them, galloping on either side of me like out-riders escorting some Royal vehicle, insisted on me running backwards and forwards across the open ground that lay behind our block of flats. It was uneven, and covered with weeds and clumps of wiry grass, and after a very short time I was panting with exhaustion and streaming with sweat. No doubt the numerous ice cream cones and other sweets I had so recently consumed did little to improve my stamina, but whenever I attempted to stop, my companions urged me on with wild cries: 'Keep going, boy, you gotta be tough for this game. You're not really tired,' and so on, until I sullenly forced myself to fresh efforts. Truly, the mind of a boy, or at least the minds of these particular boys, worked in strange ways. All their efforts were directed towards inducing me, their champion, to engage in a bloodthirsty fight which they wanted me to win, and yet they were quite prepared to half kill me with utter fatigue only a few minutes before I entered the lists on their behalf. I can only conclude that at that age, the boundaries separating reality from make-believe are not clearly defined. Or perhaps, unlike adults, they were capable of enjoying the best of both worlds, transmuting a situation that was essentially unpleasant into an innocent game.

But at last the moment came when my patience was exhausted, and I stubbornly refused to participate in any further demonstrations of athletic prowess. By this time, we had succeeded in getting well away from our base, and now the four of us sat down on the grass and prepared to consider the immediate future. It was almost dark, and as a chill autumn wind rustled the leaves, a sudden gloom descended upon us. None of them seemed to find it easy to speak, and I noticed that they avoided looking at me directly. All of us realized that the time for make-believe was over, and that we had now to confront the practical implications of the situation. After a while, we rose unwillingly to our feet and trooped slowly back towards home. My friends instinctively drew away from me, and I was suddenly conscious of being alone and thoroughly scared. As we approached South Broadway, my heart sank even lower as I heard Felix's raucous voice shouting in the distance. Lights shone from the windows of our block of flats, and the noise of passing traffic became increasingly audible.

Suddenly Emerson Nine detached himself from the group and prepared to vanish into the gloom. 'I'll go and tell him,' he muttered, and in another second his small figure disappeared at a fast trot. We had reached the open space beside the building, dark except for the light from a single bulb projecting from the brickwork above our heads. I stood indecisively in the shadow, glancing uneasily around me. My brother and Jack Kavan could not have been far away, but for the moment they were invisible and I felt completely deserted by God and man. I could not guess what would happen in the course of the next few minutes, and this uncertainty greatly increased my misery. Would Felix burst on me from the gloom, or would he first collect a couple of his torpedoes, and then march forward like a general at the head of his staff? Or would he simply ignore my challenge as something beneath contempt? But this period of suspense did not last much longer.

Some distance away from the dark street, came the sound of heavy boots running rapidly across the pavement. A familiar voice shouted, 'He wants a fight does he? OK, let's give him a fight,' and a moment later, head down, like a small bull charging into an arena, Felix rushed towards me. He did not see me for a few seconds, and came to an abrupt halt, turning his head from side to side. And then he saw me, his body stiffened, his fists clenched, and with a final roar, he lowered his bullet head and flung himself upon me. I had no time to do anything except punch, and try to keep myself on my feet. All I can remember of the next minute was the violent impact of his hard, young body, the smell of sweat, and a flurry of fists. This scrambling, panting rough-house seemed to go on for quite some time, and then, unexpectedly, he began to give ground. His punches became increasingly wild, as he retreated unwillingly, inch by inch, towards the brick wall behind him. I hit him hard somewhere on the left side of his jaw, and he faltered momentarily, staggering as he attempted to regain his balance. He lowered his fists, and for the fraction of a second I saw his chin, exposed and vulnerable, straight in front of me. Fear, and a kind of madness took possession of me. I stepped forward and hit him with all my strength. The force of the blow sent him reeling backwards stumbling and slipping, until his back struck the wall, his legs shot forward, and he collapsed in a forlorn heap. Muffled sounds of applause reached me from somewhere on my left, but all I could do was to stand transfixed with horror, staring down at my fallen enemy.

I find it difficult, even now, after a gap of fifty years, to describe what I did next. The situation was simple enough: Felix was down, and almost out, and I had certainly licked him fairly and squarely. All I had to do now was wait until, still half dazed, he strove to regain his feet, and then knock him down again. Alternatively, as the rules for such fights were extremely elastic, I could have jumped on him while he was still down, and completed the job so efficiently begun.

Instead, after a hesitation that lasted three or four seconds, I suddenly swung around and ran for my life, heading for the safety of home. Why I did this I do not know. I wish I could say that I believed half a dozen of his fellow roughs were approaching to avenge him, or that I thought I had killed him, and was consequently seized with uncontrollable terror, but I cannot honestly plead either of these excuses. All that I do remember is a sensation of sick horror; I just didn't want to fight any more, and so, in opposition to the accepted code, I wanted to get myself as far away from the scene as I possibly could. I pelted round the flank of the building, reached the pavement, and headed like a homing pigeon for the front door. Unfortunately, a couple of workmen, dressed in grimy overalls, were manoeuvring a long ladder through the doorway, and I was forced to wait, chafing and miserable, for perhaps half a minute before the exit was cleared.

If I was a pacifist, Felix was not, and as I pushed my way into the hall he shot around the corner. The entrance hall was relatively cramped, with a line of post boxes fitted with electric buttons projecting from one side of it. In these surroundings the fight started all over again, and once more I did the better job. His back was towards the row of post boxes, and every time I hit him, his close-cropped bullet head struck one or other of the buttons, causing bells to ring in half a dozen flats. Again, he went down, this time on his hands and knees directly below me, and now, gripped by an overwhelming desire to end the whole affair once and for all, I was on the point of striking a last blow on the back of his neck when the staircase was suddenly filled with outraged tenants. There were shrill cries from the women, and enraged rumblings from the men: 'Call the cops, for Christ's sake, these bloody kids should be taught a lesson.'

And that was the end of the affair. My friends congratulated me, but their voices lacked complete conviction. They were far too courteous to mention it, but from their point of view, it was logical enough to run away when you were getting a hiding but utter lunacy to do so when you were winning. But Felix never troubled us again, and perhaps this justified it all.

Even more unexpectedly than he had vanished, my father returned. Early one Sunday afternoon the doorbell rang, and there he was, tall and bronzed, surrounded by bulging suitcases and a huge trunk. The taxi-driver who had helped him to carry up his luggage was disappearing down the stairs, as father and mother faced each other across the threshold. She had become very pale, but her eyes shone with a light that had not been apparent for a long time. There was happiness in them, and yet a kind of hidden pain because she must have known that this strange, restless man whom she had loved for so long was destined to bring her little except suffering. They kissed briefly, and immediately he took charge of her life and all she possessed. The flat was filled with the sound of his loud, confident voice and purposeful footsteps. The smoke from his cigarettes drifted towards the ceiling, as he poured out the long saga of his adventures.

And as he sat there, talking and smoking, mother listened to him quietly, smiling responsively, nodding her head in agreement, and all the time, her eyes, speculative and a little sad, watched his face. He was relating his version of all that had happened during his long absence, but because she knew him so well, she must, I suppose, have been silently editing all he said, filling in gaps, separating the truth from the glib falsehoods. He brought back presents for all of us, a beautiful fur coat for mother that she was never able to wear because it was half a dozen sizes too large. He presented my brother and me with two violins, not toys but the genuine article, glowing with rich varnish, tuned to perfection. These instruments were of course completely wasted on both of us, nor did he ever explain why he had chosen to give them to us. My sister, who was then about one year old, received an enormous box of liqueur chocolates, which mother hurriedly concealed. He looked exactly the same, perhaps a little thinner, but there was something in his eyes, a secretive expression that I had not noticed before.

We gathered that the Dixie Flyer had turned out a complete failure. He spoke of it now as though it belonged to the distant past, and it was clear that the task of explaining its collapse bored him to extinction. Such facts as did emerge indicated that the South African public were a conservative lot, unwilling to experiment with an unknown make of car, and that the performance of the Flyer had fallen far short of his expectations. We never did succeed in learning whether he had actually managed to sell a single car during those early months in Cape Town, and he was obviously disinclined to discuss such academic niceties. Half a dozen large, glossy publicity photographs, some of which had presumably appeared in the local press, were all that was left of this ill-fated venture. These pictures depicted the Dixie Flyer, shining and new, standing beside a large statue, with my father leaning over the wheel in a nonchalant pose.

Apparently the Dixie Flyer and all it entailed had soon been forgotten in favour of other, more exotic interests. He spoke of a long journey through the bush in search of a fabulous copper mine which turned out to exist only in imagination. He described the wonders of new, rich cities that had sprung into existence with unbelievable rapidity. He had picked up a smattering of Afrikaans, mostly obscene phrases, and some of these I still remember. He seemed to have travelled for thousands of miles, sometimes by train or car but also on foot, walking for days across the immensity of the veldt, and camping at night under the stars. 'It's a rich country, full of amazing possibilities,' he declared enthusiastically, 'but those damned Dutchmen lack the imagination to make the most of it.' He talked deep into the night, and the next morning, because of his presence, everything was changed. His tall, restless figure dominated our cramped surroundings, his clothes lying in an untidy heap, the odour of tobacco permeating each room. Anna, usually voluble and assertive, became silent when he appeared, and little Mary looked at him with wondering curiosity.

The following afternoon he departed to report his return to Duncan Brothers, and when he got back late that evening he was angry and depressed. His reception at Duncans had been cold, and after a prolonged wrangle he had quarrelled furiously with the directors. They pointed out that his African jaunt had cost the firm rather more than fifteen thousand dollars, but added that they had no intention of asking for his resignation. Nevertheless, they were far from pleased, and stipulated that they would only continue to employ him if it was definitely understood that he should in the future confine himself to his normal duties, and exclude once and for all any further thought of impossible Eldorados.

Most people might well have considered that these were not unreasonable terms, but not my father. He retorted that while it was true that the Dixie Flyer had proved a loser, he had soon discovered another even more lucrative enterprise which would not only have wiped out his losses but shown a large profit had the firm possessed the courage to back his judgement. I was never able to understand the exact details of his grievance, but apparently he had stumbled across a fabulous opportunity for negotiating a fool-proof deal which should have instantly produced a profit large enough to cover several times over whatever had been lost on the Dixie Flyer. I seem to recall that sisal was the commodity involved, and he had sent a cable to Duncan Brothers, explaining the position and asking for something like thirty thousand dollars. But instead of arranging immediately for this amount to be credited to his account at a Cape Town bank, Duncan Brothers had dithered for so long that at last this golden opportunity had slipped away.

'The bloody idiots just lacked the guts to trust my judgement,' said my father indignantly. 'And then, after we had lost something like a certain hundred thousand as a direct consequence of their damn stupidity, they have the infernal cheek to whine about the failure of the Dixie Flyer.' It did not seem to occur to him that Duncan Brothers could hardly be blamed for displaying a certain reluctance to trust his judgement in view of the considerable sums they had already lost. He was convinced he had been the victim of rank injustice. During the three months that followed, his relations with the firm became increasingly acrimonious, and none of us was particularly surprised when he finally decided to leave them. This decision was to have far-reaching and tragic consequences, and indeed represented a landmark in both his and the family's fortunes. It marked the moment when he finally discarded even the semblance of security and routine and drifted into a dimension of nomadic eccentricity. Never again was he to be employed by a reputable firm. From then on, like an unsuccessful pirate roaming the Seven Seas in search of whatever booty came his way, he was to experiment with a score of extraordinary enterprises, each one more absurd than the last.

Our last two years in the USA were a cross between a nightmare and a prolonged ride on the big dipper at a funfair. My unfortunate mother, and to a lesser degree, the rest of the family, could only watch my father's lunatic course towards ever-increasing disaster in stupefied amazement. He got a whole series of makeshift, ridiculous jobs, none of which lasted more than a few weeks. He joined a public relations firm, attempted to sell fountain pens, and at one point actually became a night watchman in a large factory. All these efforts proved equally abortive, chiefly because he found it impossible to accept authority in any form. Within two days of becoming a salesman, he would insist on telling the sales manager exactly how to do his work. Even in the relatively sedentary role of a night watchman, he lost no time in criticizing the various duties he was expected to perform. Instead of complying with established routine, he suggested an entirely fresh approach, and was astonished and furious when the company declined to have themselves made over.

In the meantime we became increasingly hard up, and soon had to face the humiliation of losing many of our prize possessions. Our living room was ornamented with an enormous tiger skin, its head beautifully mounted and it was sold for two hundred dollars. In this fashion, one article after another disappeared. My mother watched the process with mournful resignation. When she attempted to remonstrate, father would assure her glibly that we would soon be in a position to replace everything we had lost.

And now he took to going out late at night, returning exhausted and dishevelled at dawn. With shocked disbelief, my mother was told that he had joined a syndicate of bootleggers, who specialized in smuggling hundreds of cases of illicit whisky from the West Indies. As these activities were normally controlled by powerful gangs, the operation was likely to incur the wrath of both the police and the mobsters, who naturally sought to discourage amateur attempts to invade their territory. Nevertheless, supported by two characters, a West Indian and a young, reckless Irishman named Gorman, my father was confident of his fool-proof system, which was sure to leave him the richer by many thousands of dollars. This plan proved as unsuccessful as everything else. Instead of returning with pockets bulging with hundred-dollar bills, he was compelled to admit sadly that one of his accomplices had stolen his wallet containing five hundred dollars, and that the promised consignment was never delivered. I'm sure that nothing except unbelievable luck kept him out of jail, and we heard later that Gorman had been arrested. Of course, in those days, bootlegging was accepted by a large part of the American public as a highly commendable amateur sport, but it failed to improve my father's resources.

As our finances dwindled, we left Yonkers and moved into a cramped apartment on University Avenue in the Bronx. My father's adventures in the USA were rapidly drawing to a close. I cannot now remember the exact progression of all that followed. So much happened so quickly, that it is difficult to separate one sordid event from another. I know that at one stage my father was on the run for a period of several weeks. Presumably the cops were on his tail but, if so, he succeeded in eluding them. In those days he could only contact my mother with extreme stealth. They both knew that our phone was tapped, and I remember my mother telling me years later that he adopted the ruse of speaking in Hindustani whenever he had to call her. Apparently New York's Finest listened to these conversations with mounting fury. They had men who could understand Italian, Russian, Yiddish, Greek, Romanian, German and Mexican, but not a single soul in the entire police force had ever come across anything as outlandish as Hindi. It was all rather like a nightmare, and in the finish my mother contracted pneumonia and had to be removed to hospital. Heaven knows who took charge of Mary, but both my brother and I were handed over to the care of the State of New York.

A thin, weary, middle-aged man appeared one afternoon and led us to a prim, white building somewhere around 32nd Street. Inside was a long counter, behind which sat two women busily engaged with files and letters. There was a whispered conversation and the man gave us a disillusioned smile as he vanished through the door. A plump, homely woman steered us towards a desk beyond the counter. She pushed a pile of empty envelopes and an assortment of printed forms in front of us. She was friendly but impersonal, and I had the feeling that she had been through this ritual many times before. 'Go on, kids,' she said indulgently, 'just fold those letters up and shove them into the envelopes, and here's some candy to keep your mind on your work.' She produced a massive slab of chocolate, removed the wrapper with a quick flick of her fingers, and placed it neatly between us. By then it must have been about 4.30 and for the next three and a half hours we obediently disposed of the envelopes and munched chocolate. At eight o'clock we were ushered into a tidy, antiseptic room behind the office. Four small, very clean beds that looked as though they had stepped directly out of the pages of Goldilocks awaited our arrival. Another woman, this time in nurse's uniform, welcomed us with smooth efficiency. She seemed determined to give us a bath, but after hearing that both of us had already gone through this formality, rather unwillingly decided to exempt us. We were put into clean pyjamas, the lights were lowered and soon afterwards I, at least, fell into a deep sleep. I was awakened some time in the small hours by the sound of a violent scuffling outside the door. A rich Irish brogue bellowed, 'Get in there, you young bastard,' and in another second the figure of a dishevelled youth of about fourteen shot across the threshold. He had a lean, yellow face, a mass of black hair, and was breathing heavily. The nurse instantly appeared and beckoned him towards the bathroom, but as he stumbled past my bed our eyes met. 'What are you in for?' I whispered curiously, to which he replied easily, 'Dese Police bums just framed me for stealin' women's dresses.' With this single sentence he disappeared into the white-tiled bathroom, and I cannot remember seeing him again.

The following morning we were taken to the Juvenile Court. The massive, somewhat forbidding buildings included half a dozen floors, the first two occupied by numerous court rooms which carried out their business behind locked doors. The floors above were used to accommodate scores of disgruntled, shabby youths waiting to be summoned to the courts below. Collected here were the authentic products of a great city's outcast population. These boys were Italians, Irish, Greeks, not to mention a dozen other nationalities from every part of Europe and the Near East. They were all products of the slums, of the crowded, savage streets, and most of them were guilty of theft, assault and suchlike misdemeanours. A considerable proportion of them could hardly read or write, but they all spoke in the special dialect of Brooklyn and the East Side. They drifted forwards and backwards between the broken chairs and long grimy tables, with the nonchalance of those who are completely at home.

For the next eight hours my brother and I did our best to adjust ourselves to this strange limbo. At intervals a man would hurry across the threshold and bellow a series of names, 'Caprioni ... Sullivan ... O'Brien ... Stanislaus ...' summoning them to the courts below. My brother and I were regaled with bloodcurdling stories of the miseries that awaited us. It appeared that our final destination might be one of a dozen institutions in various parts of the country. One of the boys displayed an incomprehensible animosity. Others proffered confused and contradictory advice. In the space of that long day we learnt a great deal about the dark under-belly of New York. But although these young criminals were boastful and talkative, they were also capable of genuine loyalties and unexpected generosity. We succeeded in adjusting ourselves to their world with surprising ease.

We were not, either then or later, compelled to appear in one of these courts. I suppose that as neither of us had been enterprising enough to break any sort of law, our presence was not considered necessary while an order was granted naming us as wards of the City of New York. As the afternoon dragged on, the boys became increasingly bored and quarrelsome. There were several fights, and one particularly rebellious youth was severely slapped and punched by an official. When evening came, about thirty of us, including several girls, were led downstairs. We were herded into a coach, the engine roared, and in another moment we were in rapid motion. It was dark and very cold, but the city blazed with lights and movement. The coach lurched across Broadway, garish neon signs danced like the Northern Lights above the skyscrapers, but we soon left the glitter and the crowds behind us. Now there was nothing outside but the cold darkness, and as my companions started to sing, my heart sank lower and lower. The journey seemed to last for a long time. After we had been travelling for well over an hour, I caught a fleeting glimpse of the Hudson river. The water looked dark and menacing under the winter stars, but very soon we turned sharply, and the river was left behind us.

The singing faltered and there was a sense of uneasy anticipation: we were nearing the end of our travels. The coach lost speed, then lurched to a sudden halt. Outside the frosted window, I could just see a massive building surrounded by dense pinewoods. A dim light issued from an open doorway, but otherwise the place seemed completely dark. The coach doors opened, and we piled out unwillingly into the damp gloom. I noticed that as the line of boys advanced, two men stood watchfully on either side of the column, apparently to prevent any ideas of a sudden dash for the woods.

My heart sank still lower once we had crossed the threshold. Guttering gas jets illuminated a large stone-flagged ante-room which looked exactly like something from the pages of Edgar

70

Allan Poe. We were ushered into another dim room, lined with a series of shelves, stacked with garments which looked neither very new nor very clean. Astonishingly enough, the thin, elderly woman in charge of this domain turned out to be English. We were ordered to undress, our clothes were removed and in their place we were supplied with the kind of clothing attributed to Huckleberry Finn on the banks of the Mississippi. For some reason this transformation really scared me, and the conviction that I was now an inmate of a real prison was not easy to dislodge. Arrayed in threadbare overalls and check shirts, we were now marched into a huge, cold refectory. Supper consisted of a mug of unspeakable cocoa and a minute portion of fish pie. After this formality, hungry and shivering with cold, we were directed into a damp, odoriferous room equipped with several showers. A bulky young Negro of about eighteen shouted threats and orders as the boys, in separate batches, stepped naked under the gushing hot water. Long shadows flickered across the walls and floor, producing a scene I have never been able to forget.

Finally, scrubbed and harried, we were guided through interminable dim passages and left in a vast, untidy dormitory. Here we were each given a long, white cotton nightshirt, and instructed to fold the clothes we were wearing into a neat bundle. These bundles were then collected and placed one on top of the other in a small room outside, which was immediately locked securely. I soon learnt that the object of this was to eliminate any possibility of escape during the night. For some reason, this ultimate and unexpected humiliation shook me badly, and I climbed into my narrow iron cot overwhelmed by the shadows of many dark misgivings.

We were to spend a total of rather more than three months, including Christmas, in these penal surroundings. It was not a pleasant experience and yet, despite the fact that I was always hungry, frequently terrified, and sometimes acutely miserable, the surprising fact is that I also achieved moments of real happiness. I was at the receiving end of so much that was new and strange that my perception, my ability to absorb life at every pore, was stretched to its fullest capacity. I learnt the basic facts of sex from an Irish boy, much older than myself, who clearly revelled in the task of destroying what was left of my innocence.

He described with immense gusto how he had ravished his sister under the kitchen table, dwelling lovingly on each gory detail. Seen through his eyes, the sex act seemed more like butchery than an expression of anything even distantly related to affection. I listened to this interpretation with a sensation of horror and disgust that left me almost physically sick. As far as I knew, he was telling the truth; there was no other source of information immediately available, and I can only wonder now that this initiation failed to produce permanent psychological damage.

I believe now that the horrors contained in those three months represent a kind of watershed in the history of my vagrant youth. Inwood – the name of the institution – marked the lowest rung in the ladder that had led inexorably downward. In it all the fears and uncertainties which had dogged my life achieved an accumulated force, a finality of expression. It was the end of the line. And yet even here there were moments of warmth and unexpected generosity which will never leave my memory. These young hoodlums were warm and responsive. They might steal from unguarded shops, break open parked cars, and engage in bloodthirsty battles with the cops, but these hobbies did not imply a complete lack of moral values. Their code bore little resemblance to the standards of the Establishment, and yet they had a code which most of them accepted without reservations. They would not sneak on a friend or steal from one of their own, and they were capable of displaying both sincerity and generosity. I came to look upon them as real friends, particularly a tall Italian youth known as Scorpio. He was restless and enterprising, with an infectious laugh and a highly developed gift of the gab. With him as our ally nobody dared molest my brother and me. Unfortunately, I only knew him for a couple of months because after that he was removed to one of the Corrective Farms a long way from New York.

It became intensely cold early that year. The snow fell heavily, and in a matter of hours, Inwood was surrounded by silent white drifts. I remember standing every evening, cold and forlorn, peering out of the window at the dead winter landscape. All around were the sounds of loud voices and raucous laughter, but I was lost in a private dream in which hunger and homesickness struggled for supremacy. Outside the window the deep snow, bluish white under the moonlight, lay smooth and untouched below the shadowy pines. It was indescribably beautiful, like a scene from a fairy story, and this dark, slightly sinister vision left an impression on my mind which I can never forget.

In some way a large book entitled *The Holiday Annual* had come into my possession. I don't know how I got hold of it; possibly I had removed it from our bookshelves at home when I set out on my travels; but in Inwood it proved a treasure beyond price. Lost in the colourful interior of Greyfriars, that improbable English Public School, I followed the adventures of Tom Merry and Billy Bunter with rapt attention. I escaped from the presence of the young delinquents reared on the sidewalks of New York into an even more incongruous world in which the Upper Fifth, the Shell, the leisurely struggles of the cricket field seemed all-important. I re-read these stories dozens of times, and even now the howls of the wretched Billy Bunter – 'Let me go, you beasts, ugh, yaroo, bam' – remind me instantly of that alien winter.

Some time towards the end of January my mother appeared, and in her company we walked for the last time down the long, musty corridors and out to freedom. Now our brief contact with the New World was drawing to a close. For a few weeks the family was reunited in a comfortable flat facing Central Park. In some mysterious way, my father seemed to have achieved a reconciliation with the forces of the law. I had no idea, then or later, of the exact reasons for his brief role as a fugitive pursued by the New York cops. There must have been various charges – bootlegging, evading arrest, and possibly jumping bail – hanging over his head. How he induced the New York courts to forget these breaches of the law, I shall never know. I rather suspect that by then Manhattan had had more than enough of him. Probably the prosecuting officials gave him the choice of standing trial or leaving the USA by the first available boat. They might well have decided that any arrangement which guaranteed his permanent removal was a relief which justified unusual concessions. However this may be, it was now clearly understood that our sojourn in the States was coming to an end.

Once more I found myself aboard ship. It was a cold, grey afternoon as I stood on the deck, looking down at the dark line of the wharves. The waters of the harbour were dull and lifeless, and I remembered how different it had seemed that evening five years ago when I saw it for the first time. A chunky New York tug, straining ferociously, pulled us clear of the dock, the steel cable which connected us to the stern of the tug was suddenly released and disappeared with a splash into the greasy water. Our ship shuddered, and as the screws revolved, its bulk began to move towards the sea. We were heading east towards blazing sunlight, but on that frozen afternoon the fact seemed hardly believable.

8

We must have returned to India some time late in 1923 or early in 1924. The voyage back was much less eventful than the terrors and vicissitudes we had experienced on board the *City of Lahore*, and yet, inevitably, it was not entirely lacking in the unforeseen. Our ship ran aground in the Suez Canal and remained firmly stuck to the mud. Despite the efforts of two powerful tugs, and the outraged clamour and gesticulations of the French pilot, we succeeded in blocking the channel with quite devastating efficiency for over eight hours.

After the Canal, it was Karachi, and straight on to Bombay where the voyage ended. I have a dim picture of the family waiting apathetically in an enormous warehouse for the customs authorities to give us a clearance. Something like twenty-five years later, I was to stand in this same twilit space, consumed with terror and uncertainty, preparing to embark on yet another voyage.

My father installed us in a small, rather seedy hotel which stood within a hundred and fifty yards of the harbour, and we remained in Bombay for the next two months.

I loved it all, and still recall my contact with that sea-bound sun-dazzled city with almost perfect content. But while I gloried in freedom and novelty, the fortunes of the family were sinking ever lower. India has a long memory, and though my father had been away for five years it had not forgotten him. He found it impossible to secure a post in any of the large European firms with offices nearby. Never a patient man, he met these rebuffs with uncontrolled fury. Once again he remained invisible, sometimes for several days, and eventually he disappeared altogether, explaining that he had heard of a fabulous job somewhere in Delhi.

When more than a week had elapsed without her either seeing or hearing from him, my mother was compelled to realize she had been deserted. With no cash to speak of, three children, and a constantly increasing hotel bill, her position was desperate, but she devised a plan which would at least provide us with temporary food and shelter. She wrote to her aunt, then the Sister Superior of an order of Roman Catholic nuns in Calcutta, explaining her predicament. In her reply this nun suggested that we should all travel to Calcutta where my mother would be offered a teaching job in the convent under her supervision. This sounded promising enough, but the offer included several qualifications which made it far from agreeable. It appeared that the kindly Sisters were prepared to offer my mother a refuge, but this charity did not extend to her family.

The task of transporting us to Calcutta was far from simple. The long train journey, lasting several days, was both expensive and uncomfortable, and there was also the problem of meeting the hotel bill which had remained unpaid for something like six weeks. In the end, my mother had to sell her few surviving valuables, a bracelet, a necklace, and some sort of brooch, to settle her account for board and lodging, and once this was done very little remained. Using up almost her last rupee, she was able to buy the railway tickets to Calcutta, though the best we could afford was third-class transport. Our sordid compartment lacked both fans and cooling equipment and consequently we were half dead from heat and exhaustion when at last we reached our destination.

The convent proved to be relatively comfortable, and quite beautiful. The grounds were silent and spacious, surrounded by tall trees, which concealed statues of the Virgin Mary and other particularly revered saints. My mother and her family were allowed to settle down in two large airy rooms which constituted a sort of annexe to the main buildings; but the Sister Superior continued to insist that my mother would only be allowed to stay without the encumbrance of her children. Within a matter of days, my unfortunate sister Mary, pale and tearful, was placed in the charge of an ageing spinster named Miss Felloni and carted off to Darjeeling. Soon after her departure my brother and I were told that arrangements had been made to enrol us in a rather shoddy boarding school also on the outskirts of Darjeeling. Even at the age of thirteen, I was accustomed to the vicissitudes which constantly threatened our life, and I received this news without apparent emotion. But it was a change which I accepted without pleasure or hope.

St Theobald's school was run by an order of Irish Christian Brothers, big red-faced men, addicted to gusts of throaty laughter and the use of a rich brogue. When I think of that school my memory produces a picture of bleak, sodden playing fields, crowded dormitories, and ink-spattered classrooms. All around us were the great, soaring ramparts of the Himalayas, unbelievably beautiful in their lonely grandeur, but inside the school everything was mean, damp and oppressive. I suppose the sun did shine now and then, but if so it must have escaped my notice. All I can remember is an unending drizzle, with patches of grey mist scurrying across the sky, driven forward by an icy wind. Everything about the place seemed wet and unhealthy, a coating of slippery fungus encrusting floors and furniture, the smell of damp and mildew ever present. It must have been the monsoon period when my brother and I went to the school, because every three or four hours the drizzle would change into a torrential downpour.

The school catered for about two hundred boys, mostly Anglo-Indians, though there was also a smattering of country-born whites. Discipline was enforced by the use of a sinister strap about eighteen inches long, which consisted of a whale-bone base enclosed in black leather. This instrument was applied to either the hands or bottom, and though I was only to remain at this school for a period of six or seven months, I must have received at least a hundred strokes from it during that time. The boys went to Mass every morning and on Sunday there was evening Benediction as well as a lengthy morning service.

It was not a good school, even judged by the standards of its time, and I hated it with a deep and unchanging hatred from the moment I first saw it. This may well seem a little hard to understand. After all I had survived several of the toughest American schools, and even the horrors of Inwood, with something approaching philosophical resignation; but there was something about Theobald's that produced a special repulsion that I had never experienced before. I can't pretend that the Irish Brothers were particularly unkind; in fact, they often treated me with a leniency which implied understanding and even sympathy for my predicament. But their contact with the boys was necessarily limited, and nothing they could do could change my instinctive rejection of all that the place represented.

For the first time in my life, I learnt the bitterness of total isolation. I can remember walking alone across that rain-swept deserted playing field, for hours at a stretch. I would walk very fast, head bowed against the force of an icy wind, a hundred and fifty yards in one direction, and then back over the same ground. I developed in time a sort of personal yoga, which allowed me to escape from the torments of reality into a dimension of dreams. In this fashion I was able to forget the humiliations, the petty restrictions, the ghastly food and the hostility of most of my companions, as I disappeared down a psychological hole that led to a private world of happiness and security.

After the rough-necks of New York with their vitality and fierce insistence on personal liberty, my present companions seemed tame and colourless, accepting the arbitrary pressures of authority with contemptible docility. These boys collected holy pictures, vied with each other for the honour of serving at Mass, and toadied to the masters with a servility that I could never hope to emulate. They would sit in a circle, brandishing their holy pictures, arguing about the respective merits of incomprehensible saints, and as I listened to their soft chee chee accents, I felt like a creature from another planet. Naturally enough, they reacted instinctively to this mistrust with dislike and rejection. According to their simple minds, my convictions bordered on anarchy, and as time passed it became increasingly evident that the task of turning me into a good Catholic boy was not going to be easy.

I was in what was then called the Sixth Standard, which was

presided over by a bulky, middle-aged man named Mr Callow. Mr Callow wore a ragged, ginger moustache and a considerable paunch. He had thinning hair, glazed, bad-tempered blue eyes, and a complexion of such a florid hue that apoplexy seemed a constant menace.

I was told that Mr Callow had spent his entire life teaching in this shabby school tucked away on a Himalayan ridge. He was unmarried, and as a layman living on the fringe of a closely-knit religious community, his life must have been appallingly lonely. I don't suppose he had spoken to a woman in years, apart from our singing teacher, an ancient, bony spinster with a thin, bad-tempered mouth and a blotchy skin – nicknamed the bitch cobra by the boys.

This deprivation may have explained certain oddities of behaviour with which I was to become only too familiar during the months we were to spend together. During class, as a general rule, he bullied, scolded and nagged with ferocious zest. Crimson with rage, he would lumber across the room, and within minutes, two or three culprits would be dragged to the front, ordered to hold out their hands, and receive the attentions of his dreaded strap. But there was always at least one boy, or sometimes two, on whom his wrath never descended. These favourites were immune, and evoked a response that was completely unlike his normal behaviour. In their presence, that angry, swollen face would suddenly change into a soft, smirking mask, from which his blood-shot eyes shone with repulsive liquid sentimentality.

His current weakness was a thin, effeminate boy named Percy Hookey. This character was both conceited and a sneak, and was greatly disliked by the majority of his companions, though few of them had the courage to show it. But he was no mean actor, and immediately Mr Callow hove in sight, was able to put on a performance that would have instantly got him a job as a female impersonator. He would flutter his eyelashes, simper with girlish abandon and in general behave like a new recruit to a sultan's harem. Mr Callow would view these antics with undisguised pleasure, smiling fatuously, his eyes glittering with unconcealed approbation. At such moments he would express himself in a peculiar form of baby talk, patting the boy's cheek with his large fat hand. Hookey would pout and blush, wriggling his behind with such skill that Mr Callow was goaded to fresh excesses.

My first intimation of this flirtatious by-play occurred soon after I had joined his class. Slouching disconsolately over my desk, staring sadly at a cheap copy of Scott's *Lay of the Last Minstrel*, I was striving to memorize the lines:

> If you would view fair Melrose aright
> Pray visit it by the pale moonlight

when suddenly my reveries were interrupted by the sound of a mawkish, unnatural voice, intoning playfully 'Wicked little Hookey needs a slap.' Looking up in disgusted amazement, I saw Mr Callow, his fat face creased into a leer, bending over the wriggling, simpering boy. The expression on my face must have showed my feelings only too clearly, and unfortunately at that exact second the infatuated man glanced in my direction and our eyes met. It was a moment of truth that neither of us could forget.

For me, everything about that school was repressive and unhappy. The teaching methods never went beyond a prolonged, boring insistence on cramming. Nothing was discussed or explained. We were merely called upon to absorb, word by word, great masses of print, seldom glimpsing more than a tiny fraction of the real meaning that lay behind the text. In this fashion, we memorized, verse by verse, all the four Gospels, every line of Scott's *Lay of the Last Minstrel*, and the whole of *The Tempest*, including lengthy, incomprehensible notes. We spent five hours every day, ostensibly receiving instruction in the classroom, and another four hours which were theoretically devoted to prep. After a while, unwillingly, I actually began to enjoy large chunks of Scott's romantic poem, and even certain selections of Shakespeare but I don't think this applied to many of the others. Few of them had ever attempted to read for pleasure, and they expressed their detestation of Scott and Shakespeare in words of colourful obscenity.

The boys were strangely apathetic, almost lifeless. Held in subjection by the strap and cane, they showed little of the spontaneous high spirits normally found amongst boys. The system had succeeded so well in crushing thought and enterprise, that on one level their capacity to mature seemed to have been almost completely destroyed. Their interests were confined to hockey and religion, and they were hardly aware that another wider world lay beyond the mountains. And yet this infantile obsession was mixed with something else that was not in the least childlike, a quality of fatalistic wisdom that seemed as old as India itself. Sneaking and tale-bearing were encouraged, which led inevitably to an atmosphere of distrust and cunning. My processes of thought seemed to them both dangerous and sacrilegious, and for the first time in my life I found myself without a single friend.

The food was so bad that, despite the pangs of hunger, I could seldom bring myself to eat it. It consisted of vast portions of rice and curry suitable to the tastes of the poorest Indian coolies, along with the kind of rations that were probably served in His Majesty's Navy about the time of Trafalgar. For breakfast each boy received two enormous round biscuits about seven inches in diameter, in addition to a large mug of watery tea, served from gigantic tin jugs. These biscuits were so hard that only those with the strongest teeth were able to chew them without first softening them by a process of prolonged dunking. The luncheon menu consisted of huge platefuls of sloppy rice, mixed with very hot curry. This food was served by a very fat disillusioned Indian bearer, known to the boys as Billy Bunter. He would plunge up and down the long refectory, gripping four plates in each hand in such a way that his large brown thumbs were embedded in the greasy mass contained in the topmost plate. During meals one of the brothers, armed with a long cane, marched up and down between the tables, exhorting and threatening with the vehemence and skill born of long practice. The biscuits reappeared for supper, but on this occasion they were coated with some unknown substance that was politely called margarine. And for this last meal, tea was replaced by a loathsome brown liquid that I believe was supposed to be cocoa.

The part of the day that I disliked most was about 6 p.m., when a gong sounded to summon us to supper. The vast playing field would be engulfed in a dim, bleak twilit pallor. All two hundred of us formed a long straggling line, flanked by a retinue of brothers watching eagle-eyed for a victim on whom to vent their displeasure.

Marshalling the entire school often meant that the earlier arrivals had to wait in the cold darkness for as long as ten or fifteen minutes. Most of the boys wore heavy overcoats, but as neither my brother nor I possessed such a garment, all we could do was shiver miserably as an icy Tibetan wind buffeted our thin bodies. Beyond the line, shrouded in gloom, the ugly bulk of the school waited like a prison, and to add a final macabre touch, this was the time when the jackals skulking in the wet undergrowth, started to howl in a lunatic chorus.

Behind us was a long row of toilets, like a string of battered bathing huts. Early stars, frozen and remote, shone down on us from the dark arch of the sky. The minutes dragged slowly by, until at last somebody shouted an order and with an unutterable sense of relief we all marched forward.

The bad food, loneliness and other miseries soon began to affect my health. For the first time in my life I felt really sick, losing a stone in weight and suffering from a constant sensation of listless fatigue. Due, no doubt, to some kind of vitamin deficiency, large sores appeared on my legs and thighs which refused to heal. The school disdained the use of doctors, and consequently these wounds were dressed at infrequent intervals by a Bhutia pharmacist using techniques that had probably not changed much since the time of the Indian Mutiny. He would first unbandage the infected area, and then, using something that looked like a large paintbrush, proceed to clean the wounds with a generous supply of raw iodine. This therapy was extremely painful and it is perhaps not surprising that I avoided him as often as I could.

A considerable part of my distress could be traced to the fact that, after the first couple of weeks, I always felt slightly dirty and unkempt. We were only allowed a bath once a week, which ceremony was carried out with the maximum of noise and discomfort in batches of fifty. Complete nudity was not considered permissible and the boys had to wear skimpy shorts, known as 'jungiers', during the entire course of their ablutions. They were lined up, facing huge metal tubs that looked rather like horse troughs, while a watchful brother marched backwards and forwards, exhorting them to wash their bums and behind their ears.

I cannot remember a single moment of real happiness in all the dreary months I spent at that school. There were times, fleeting minutes and even hours, when I was able to recapture my old content, but these only occurred when I succeeded in escaping in my mind, or through a book, from reality. Pacing endlessly across the wet, deserted playing field, I forgot the shoddy class-rooms and the soaring, aloof grandeur of the Himalayas, and returned to those happy months when I had been free to wander beside the waters of Bombay harbour. Soaked in dazzling sun-light, the smell of the sea in my nostrils, I saw again the white sails of the dhows as the wind carried them towards Africa, and mingled happily with the cosmopolitan crowds that drifted be-side the waterfront. I could not often escape through books because the school library was restricted to novels of such appal-ling dullness that even my starving imagination could extract little enjoyment from them. Every other book in this library seemed to have been written by a man named Henty who special-ized in producing noxious 'wholesome' stories thickly laced with historical facts. Sex and love were rigorously excluded from these narratives, and the only females allowed to appear were mothers, aunts and suchlike ennobling characters. Every now and then I did collect something readable, and these finds were hoarded like gold and re-read so often that I could almost repeat them by heart.

With the passage of time my sores disappeared and I regained a great part of my normal health; but each day increased my hatred for the school and all it represented. Then, quite suddenly, I reached a decision. I thought 'I'm going to get out of this, whatever the cost,' and instantly was conscious of a sense of re-lief, almost of happiness, as though this resolve had opened a door that had remained closed far too long.

9

I had no illusions about the difficulties that blocked my way. Decisions were relatively easy, but the task of translating them into reality was entirely different. The first and all-important question was, where could I run to? My mother and father were living in a flat in Bombay, and Bombay was over a thousand miles away from school. I should explain that my parents had come together again about eight months after their separation. My father, knowing exactly where to find my mother and inexplicably convinced that she was indeed essential to his restless, chaotic life, suddenly appeared at the Convent and within a matter of minutes had induced her to commit her life and happiness into his hands yet again. I knew that the family's financial position was extremely precarious, and that even if I succeeded in reaching Bombay the chances of being allowed to remain there were almost nil. All I was likely to receive was a series of painful home truths and a speedy return to the horrors of the school.

I decided finally, after prolonged consideration, that Bombay was out, and the question now was, where else could I hope to find refuge? I thought long and feverishly, and at last struck on what seemed a promising solution. On the voyage from New York we had met an American woman named Mrs Sprague who was coming to India to join her husband in a remote part of Assam. We had become friendly, and I recalled that she had said on more than one occasion that she would like my brother and me to spend some time with her in her lonely bungalow. I had not seen her for over a year, but I had her address somewhere, and when I remembered her thin, homely face and her patient pale blue eyes, I felt pretty sure that if she could be reached, everything might work satisfactorily.

I thought it over from every angle for a couple of days, and the more I looked at it the more determined I became to chance my luck. My first positive move was to talk it over with my brother. I slipped over to his bed one night when I was sure that we were unobserved, and shook him awake. He opened his eyes, stretched and looked at me coldly. The trouble was that we had never been very close, and even in that wretched school he had insisted on going it alone. Because of this estrangement, it was not easy to judge what his reactions were likely to be, and the only way to find out was to shove the plan under his nose and hope for the best. We stared at each other in silence for a few seconds and then he mumbled suspiciously, 'What's wrong, what's the idea of waking me up?' I bent over him, and whispered hoarsely, 'I've made up my mind to do a bunk, and the point is, will you come with me?' His eyes narrowed, and he half

83

sat up. 'Do a bunk,' he snorted incredulously, 'Why, you must be off your bloody head. Go on, push off and let me get to sleep.' 'No,' I said, still whispering, 'I've got a plan; I've got it all worked out, so just shut up for a minute and let me talk.'

He closed his eyes and let his head fall on the pillow. 'Shit,' he said, 'you must be off your nut. You know damn well you've got nowhere to run to, and in any case how the hell are you going to raise the money to get anywhere?' I outlined the project in detail, making it sound as easy as possible, but after the first minute I knew I had failed. His eyes were still open but the expression in them was cold and hard. He thought for a bit and then he said, 'It's bloody lunacy. You can count me out.' Knowing him as I did, I realized that was the end of the discussion. I was sorry, and yet in another way the prospect of working alone had its compensations.

My next move was to try to discover all I could about the route I had to cover. This was comparatively easy, as a fair proportion of the boys had parents employed by one or other of the huge Indian railway systems, and could produce the exact itinerary of every important train traversing the country with the accuracy of a timetable. After studying parts of an old diary, and re-reading the few crumpled letters from her which still remained in my possession, I was sure that Mrs Sprague lived in or near a town named Silchar, close to the frontier that divided Assam from Burma. Such information as I could glean regarding the journey that confronted me was not encouraging. The distance, judged by Indian standards, was not unusually long, but it involved several complicated changes and the necessity at one point of boarding a river steamer that sailed down the Ganges.

Reduced to its essentials, the journey involved a distance of a little over eight hundred miles. I would first have to reach Calcutta, and then board another train travelling through East Bengal as far as a station named Galundo, on the banks of the Ganges. Having got so far, I must then manage to stow away on a river steamer that sailed from Galundo to yet another station called Chandpore. The Assam mail left Chandpore at 9 p.m., and supposing I were lucky enough to get that far, was scheduled to arrive at Silchar at 8 o'clock the following morning. It all sounded fairly complicated and terrifying. I knew absolutely nothing about this part of the country, and when I heard that the railway did not extend beyond Silchar and that there was nothing further on except the virgin jungle, my heart sank even lower.

During the week that followed, by various devious means I succeeded in collecting the sum of 7 rupees, 8 annas (about 45p), a small canvas haversack, a clean shirt, several bars of chocolate, a torn map of East Bengal, and a paperback novel entitled *Sexton Blake among the Parsees*. The knowledge that my days in this loathsome school were now numbered, instantly changed everything for the better. I woke up each morning, warmed by the cheery certainty that very soon Theobald's, Mr Callow and the long boring sessions in the classroom would no longer constitute my life, and that the future, beckoning and insistent, represented escape and freedom.

Nobody, except my brother, myself and a boy named Humphries, was aware of my intentions. The three of us would discuss my plan for hours at a stretch, my brother aloof and slightly contemptuous, Humphries overflowing with enthusiasm and advice. Their part in the plot called for nothing except silence, and when at last my absence was noted, a stolid insistence that they had always been completely ignorant of what was going on in my mind. I decided finally that the following Saturday evening was a suitable time to start the great event. I reached this decision on Tuesday morning, and those last three days dragged.

At last, the morning of the great day came. I sat at my desk, exactly as I had done a hundred times before, and listened to Mr Callow ranting and raving. I even received as a sort of unrehearsed gesture of farewell, four last strokes from his sadistic black strap. At lunch I obediently consumed yet another portion of clotted rice and greasy curry. Everything was unchanged, but somehow the familiar routine seemed entirely different. That last morning and afternoon passed with extraordinary speed, but when the moment for action drew close, I would have gladly postponed it for another few hours.

My strategy of escape was simplicity itself. Just before 6 o'clock I would shut myself inside one of the grimy toilets that lined the far end of the playing field. From this rather undignified position I would be able to hear clearly the sound of the gong summoning my companions for prep. All I had to do then was to hang on for another ten or fifteen minutes until the gong sounded for the second time, and the heavy tramping of retreating feet told me that the school was marching indoors. After that it should be a push-over, involving nothing more difficult than opening a door and walking boldly into the now deserted playing field. My next objective was Kurseong Railway Station, two miles away down the mountain road, where I hoped to board the tiny Himalayan train which should carry me to Silhguri and the waiting Calcutta Mail. That large, vast train should deposit me at Calcutta around 8 o'clock the following morning. After that my plans were pretty vague, but the general idea was that I should either stow away on board a ship, or make my way somehow to Silchar and the safety of Mrs Sprague's bungalow.

I was not unduly worried by the fact that I had committed myself to travelling over a vast portion of India without the funds to buy a ticket. Long experience had taught me a dozen different ways of outwitting the efforts of troublesome guards and ticket inspectors. And in the India of those days, even if I was detected, the chances were that most soft-hearted Anglo-Indian railway officials would be reluctant to eject a European boy at some god-forsaken station.

But other, more immediate problems were on my mind that momentous evening when, at exactly ten to six, I found myself, accompanied by Humphries and my brother, standing in the chill twilight outside the line of toilets. My brother looked at me coldly, as though I were a stranger whom he never expected to see again. 'Goodbye,' he said flatly, and instantly turned his back and vanished into the gloom. Humphries was obviously gripped by the drama of the situation. He clutched my hand and shook it warmly. 'Goodbye, and good luck,' he muttered, and then he too had disappeared. I dragged open the door of the toilet, went inside, and shut the door carefully behind me. I sat down on the only available seat, and prepared myself for a long vigil. Everything seemed oddly unreal and I was not so much scared as numb and disbelieving. After that it went exactly as I had planned. When the second gong had sounded and the thud of marching feet told me that the school was heading towards the classrooms, I waited cautiously for another five minutes and then opened the door and walked boldly into the deserted playing field. In another five seconds I had rounded the dim line of lavatories and headed down the mountainside.

I went down the hillside as fast as I could; running whenever possible, walking or scrambling when the angle of the descent became more difficult. The wet bushes hampered my progress, clutching at my ankles and knees with hard thorny stalks. I slipped and scrambled through the darkness, and had almost reached the road when I fell heavily, twisting my right leg at an awkward angle. I thought at first that I had sprained my ankle, and as I slumped on the wet ground, cold leaves brushing against my face, the realization of all that such an accident would entail was too horrible to contemplate. But after a couple of minutes I managed to get back on my feet, and my spirits rose as the pain in my ankle subsided. The road was a narrow, winding track that sloped downwards between high ridges of rock, but at least it was free of unexpected hazards. My destination lay about two miles ahead, and I must have covered this distance in rather less than half an hour.

The darkness was filled with the smell of the mountains, a damp, sharp smell that was a mixture of wet jungle and running water. Nobody saw me as I hurried forward except an old Bhutia woman, bent and withered, gathering firewood by the roadside. Soon a cluster of dim lights far ahead warned me that I was nearing the station. The platform was almost empty when I reached it, but the train was in, its small, powerful locomotive puffing and steaming at the head of a long line of dimly-lit, tiny coaches. I climbed into one of them and managed to find a seat near the off window. The compartment was crammed with a collection of grizzled old planters, all Europeans, from Darjeeling. They smelt of cigars and whisky and were engrossed in a rambling conversation about hunting tigers, the current crop of tea and the injustices practised by the Government against the tea-planting fraternity.

They hardly seemed conscious of my presence, until a fat old boy sitting next to me produced a flask of whisky and offered me a drink. He seemed surprised when I refused and said disapprovingly 'You'd better learn to drink whisky, young fellow, or you'll die of malaria before you're twenty-one.' This was a generally accepted myth in those days. I was not particularly impressed, but I could not avoid eyeing a large packet of uneaten sandwiches which lay on his lap. He must have noticed the greed in my eye, because after a second or two he handed them over, saying generously, 'Go on, tuck in, I don't want the bloody things.' When I started to eat, I was so hungry that it required all my will-power not to gobble the fresh tasty food with unsightly haste.

For the next four hours the small train whistled and rocked as it slid down the steep gradients that led to the plains. In contrast with Kurseong, Silhguri was crowded and ablaze with light. There was noise and movement as hundreds of people swarmed around waiting to catch the Calcutta Mail.

Standing in the shadows, the realization that at last I was really free hit me for the first time and made me enormously happy. The mail was not due to leave for another forty-five minutes, and I decided to buy myself a cup of tea from the mobile stall further down the platform. I pushed forward confidently, savouring in advance the taste of the hot sweet liquid. And then, I saw something that brought me to an abrupt halt. Standing beside the steaming urns, wearing a long, dirty overcoat, and a battered felt hat, was the school barber. This man was a Goan named Ignatius, who knew me all too well, and his reactions once he saw me in these surroundings were only too easy to calculate. As I stood transfixed, he turned his head and glanced towards me, and I thought I saw a gleam of astonished recognition appear in his dark, protruding eyes. I swung around and hurried blindly down the platform. I saw a door on my right, and on the impulse of the moment, pushed it open and darted inside.

I looked around me, panting and confused, and realized that pure luck had led me inside the men's lavatory. A couple of swift steps took me inside one of the urinals, and I stayed there, pretending to pee, while my mind struggled furiously to cope with this unexpected disaster. One point was certain, my only hope of escape was to get far away from Ignatius and this station without the loss of a single second. He was obviously here to board the Calcutta train and until he was well out of sight my present surroundings represented the maximum of danger. There was a window at the rear of the lavatory, overlooking the open country behind the station. Its wooden shutters looked as though they had not been opened for years, but the need to do something prompted me to approach it. I pulled at the rusty bolt, and was pleasantly surprised to feel the thing move under the pressure of my fingers. The next second, the window fanned open and I found myself staring at the dark vault of the night sky.

A gentle, hot wind touched my face as I clambered over the lintel and dropped the few feet that led to temporary safety. I loped forward as rapidly as I could, leaving the station behind me. I was on a plain that extended without interruption until it reached the dim bulk of the mountains soaring upwards at the extreme limits of the horizon. I felt horribly vulnerable as I advanced deeper and deeper into the empty wilderness. The sight of a European boy marching with maniacal determination towards exactly nothing might have seemed a shade unusual in those days, but fortunately I was concealed in the kindly darkness. And the ground must not have been as flat as I expected, because when I looked back after a few minutes, the lights of the station had vanished behind some invisible hump.

It was very silent, and I was suddenly conscious of an illogical sense of fear and unease as though I was an intruder in a world that wanted no part of me. I saw a jackal, its belly almost touching the ground as it slunk into the bushes, and from somewhere above me an eerie, metallic croak denoted the presence of some invisible creature of the night. A mis-shapen half moon was rising slowly above the horizon, and the air was heavy and oppressive. There was a clump of bamboos to my right close to an outcrop of large rocks. I sat down beside the rocks and resigned myself to a long, uncomfortable night. I realized that I was very tired, and let my body slump down on the hard, parched ground. Just before I fell asleep, I remember noticing a peculiar, unpleasant odour that I was unable to identify. But I was too tired to care, and as sleep overpowered me, I remembered thinking, 'At least I'm free; at least I've got rid of that bloody school.'

I don't suppose I could have slept for more than three hours, but when I awoke the squat moon had climbed high into the sky, and everything was bathed in pale, ghostly moonlight. I pulled myself into a sitting position and fumbled in my pocket for a cigarette. And then I heard an odd rustling sound beyond the rocks, and involuntarily crouched lower behind the boulders. The rustling sound was followed by an inexplicable gobbling and scraping that seemed to come from several directions at once. There was an opening between the rocks, and lowering my head cautiously, I peered through it.

Ten yards beyond the rocks a collection of monstrous creatures formed a circle around some unknown object. There must have been thirteen or fourteen of them, each separated from the other by about a foot, positioned so accurately that they might have been figures carved out of stone.

The skin on my forehead contracted with terror. For some time, still partially dazed by sleep, I was unable to decide whether these apparitions were alive or dead, animal or human. They were apparently three or four feet in height with heavy, clumsy bodies hunched forward at a grotesque angle. Their thick, short necks dropped downwards, supporting monstrous brooding heads that seemed bowed by the weight of sinister contemplation. I was half convinced that I was the unwilling witness of some secret, corrupt ritual, performed by creatures that had stepped straight out of a nightmare. They were almost completely motionless, except that every now and then one or other of them would turn its head from side to side with a rapid suspicious movement, while the rest of their bodies remained immobile. The air was heavy with the stench of rotting flesh.

Then, as my sight gradually accustomed itself to the sickly moonlight, I suddenly realized the real significance of this ghostly scene. These creatures were neither phantoms of the night, nor unknown monsters never glimpsed before. They were vultures, seen for the first time at close quarters, gathered round the corpse of a donkey. Everything fell into focus instantly. I could even clearly see the body of the donkey, or at least what was left of it, the entrails spilling out of its yawning belly, its huge teeth exposed in a dreadful caricature of a grin.

For the next fifteen minutes, crouched behind the rocks, I watched this grotesque scene with horrified fascination. I felt like an interloper, spying on a secret world that existed beyond the range of humanity. At regular intervals one of the vultures would inflate its body, extend its enormous wings, and flap forward in a series of clumsy hops. When it reached its objective, the great, curved beak would stab and slash until it grasped a hunk of flesh. It would then return to its place in the circle and in due course another bird would repeat the ritual. I never saw more than one bird advance at a time. Apparently such movements were ordained by immutable laws.

Eventually, feeling more than a little sick, I turned round and slithered away into the darkness. When I thought it was safe, I rose to my feet and hurried away into the protective gloom. I kept on walking for several minutes, and by then I had no clear idea which way I was heading. A little later, the thought occurred to me that in the darkness I might be walking in a circle and thus suddenly find myself again confronting those unspeakable vultures. This possibility did not appeal to me at all, and I came to a standstill while I strove to make out some object that I could walk towards. At last I saw a faint gleam of greenish light somewhere in the darkness ahead. I walked towards it, but it must have been much further away than I first imagined because after a lapse of fifteen or twenty minutes it still seemed a long way off. Then, suddenly, it loomed clear and bright within a few yards of me, and I saw that it was a signal light guarding the long line of rail that led towards the station.

The platform looked empty and desolate under the dim lights and the hand of the big station clock pointed to exactly 4.30. I spent the rest of the night in the first-class waiting room, sleeping in one of the long planter's chairs which at that time were standard equipment in every waiting room in India. When I awoke at 8 o'clock, I found myself surrounded by half a dozen people, waiting to board one of the early local trains. My night in the open had left me rather the worse for wear, and my first objective was the washroom, where I tidied myself up as best I could. After that, I walked out onto the platform and brought myself a boiling hot cup of tea and two small loaves of bread. This feast, purchased from an Indian vendor, cost me the equivalent of two pence and I drank the delicious brew and ate the hot, fresh bread in full view of the passers-by. The sight of a European boy, gobbling cheap bazaar food in the middle of a crowded platform might well have shocked some of the opulent sahibs and their womenfolk, but I was too hungry to consider such niceties. But nobody seemed to question my presence on the station and with every passing minute my confidence increased. It was exhilarating to be free to do exactly as I wanted, and the knowledge that at this exact moment my brother and Humphries were marching towards their dismal classroom greatly increased the enjoyment of my hard-won freedom.

The Calcutta Mail was not due to arrive for another five hours, but I don't think that I was either bored or impatient at this enforced leisure. The bookstall consisted of a large circular contraption loaded with colourful magazines and a rich collection of crisp, new novels. I recall that Zane Grey's current Western best-seller entitled *The Thundering Herd* was prominently displayed, and that during the course of the next few hours I succeeded in reading no less than 123 pages of this dramatic novel. At regular intervals my illicit enjoyment of the story would be interrupted by the unexpected appearance of the young Hindu clerk in charge of the stall. 'It is not permitted to make use of this stall as a library. Either purchase the book, or leave it in its allotted place,' he would say disapprovingly, but as soon as his back was turned I would return to this enchanting world of six-guns and stetsons.

When the Calcutta Mail finally arrived, I carefully selected a first-class compartment; after all, as I was not paying for my ticket, there seemed no point in unnecessary economy. I waited until the very last moment and climbed rapidly aboard. Whenever the train drew into a particularly large station, where a ticket check was likely to occur, I would swiftly push open the door, leap onto the platform and mingle with the crowd, returning to my place a second before the line of carriages jerked into motion. At other times, I would conceal myself in the cramped toilet attached to each compartment and remain there until the moment of danger had passed. I suppose I can claim to know more about the interior of Indian railway toilets than any other living human being.

For the next seven hours the system seemed to work admirably, and then my luck ran out. Disaster occurred late that same evening as the Mail jerked to a halt at a large, noisy station. Almost before my feet had time to reach the platform, an enterprising ticket collector pounced upon me with the purposeful hostility of a hunting tiger. He was a short, dapper Moslem, wearing a very new blue uniform, including the official round peaked hat. His out-thrust jaw proclaimed him to be a man not easily deflected from his purpose. 'Your ticket please,' he rapped imperiously, and for once I was at a loss for words. At last I said weakly, 'I haven't got a ticket,' upon which, like a policeman making an arrest, he advanced swiftly and touched my shoulder. 'You will immediately accompany me to the station-master's office.'

Something told me that I was confronting a character not susceptible to eloquence. I thought fast. 'Look, Inspector,' I said, 'if you let me go, I'll give you half the money I have in this pocket,' and I tapped the front of my bush shirt invitingly. I was not mistaken; my opponent was capable of arriving at a split-second decision. 'How much money have you got in your pocket?' he asked, and in another minute I had sadly surrendered half my small capital.

Apart from this incident, the journey to Calcutta was uneventful. The train trickled wearily into Sealdah at 1.05 a.m. Once more I found myself standing forlornly on a long, almost deserted railway platform, but this was a big city station and even at that time a few lonely figures were drifting here and there. A group of drunken soldiers wearing kilts and white spats wandered aimlessly towards the entrance. Two Europeans in evening dress were apparently involved in a lengthy argument outside the waiting room. As I looked at them, one of the debaters suddenly staggered and sat down heavily on the hard concrete. His companion attempted to haul him to his feet, but only succeeded in falling on top of him. Calcutta, even at 1 a.m., was obviously a city rich in vitality. I felt horribly hungry, but the loss of half of my money compelled me to practise economy, and all I could afford were two cups of tea.

For the second night in succession I slept on a railway station. This time I did not sleep deeply but merely dozed fitfully, disturbed constantly by the mysterious sounds of the great city. All through the night strange people passed in and out of the waiting room. Some talked softly as though engaged in an endless argument, others cursed and sang in drunken abandon. When morning came I found myself sandwiched between a plump young Parsee and a thin nervy European woman with two small children. She seemed flurried and slightly irritated, admonishing the children in sharp sentences, constantly peering at the clock or fumbling with her luggage. A waiter from the first-class refreshment room dashed in and deposited a richly laden breakfast tray on the low table in front of her. A delicious smell of fresh coffee, hot buttered toast and bacon drifted towards my nostrils. I watched enviously as the woman opened her bag, extracted a glossy 10-rupee note, and paid the bill with haughty indifference.

'Robert, Jennifer, come on and have your breakfast,' she commanded, as she bent forward to pour out the coffee. The sight was more than I could bear; involuntarily I closed my eyes and licked my lips. At that moment, had I known the meaning of the word communist, I would certainly have become a party member with the zeal borne of instant conversion. The sound of rapidly approaching footsteps caused me to open my eyes. A tall European, breathing heavily, stood at the doorway, looking accusingly at the woman beside me. 'Come on Blanche,' he called, 'Bill's here. I told you we'd have to hurry.' The woman rose hurriedly to her feet, seized her children and disappeared onto the platform. For a minute or two I could hardly believe in this miracle that had apparently been designed to meet my special needs. Then I sprang to my feet, took possession of her chair and got down to serious eating. I consumed three cups of coffee, four fried eggs, several slices of bacon and half a dozen rounds of magnificent buttered toast, without once raising my head. When at last I surfaced, I saw that the young Parsee was watching me with undisguised astonishment.

After that, it seemed advisable to get out of the station as soon as I possibly could. Like some monster, the huge, sprawling city swallowed me at a single gulp. I felt happy but a little scared, and the realization that, amongst all these millions, not a single soul was even aware of my existence gave me a sense of loneliness that I had not experienced before. I boarded a crowded tram which rocked and jangled through the bazaars. I had been away from the city for so long that I hardly knew where I was going. But surprisingly soon old memories revived, and I began to recognize landmarks. Because the idea of stowing away on board a ship still captured my imagination, my first objective was obviously to find the river.

This proved more difficult than I anticipated. Eventually my tram stopped at Chowringhee, the centre of the European section of the city. The broad, clean road, lined with expensive shops and big hotels, stretched straight before me, as I started to walk through the morning light. I thought then that I would be able to reach the water in rather less than half an hour, but I was soon to learn that this estimate was absurdly optimistic. I skirted the park, passed the tall ornamental gates of Government House, guarded by two mounted Bengal lancers resplendent in their scarlet uniforms, without once gaining sight of my objective.

I must have been walking for nearly an hour and a half when at last a sudden gust of wind carried the smell of the river towards me. Five minutes later I was standing on a rickety wooden wharf twenty feet above the broad yellow expanse of the Hoogly. I looked across the ugly, menacing flood and felt my heart sink. This torrent of liquid mud, its surface writhing with the force of invisible currents, was totally unlike the colourful vitality of the real sea. The sharp, clean smell of salt water was replaced by the odour of slime and dirt, and except for a couple of grotesque Indian craft wallowing downstream, not a single ocean-going vessel was visible. I realized then that my long journey had been completely pointless; the kind of ships I had in mind were berthed at the docks several miles from where I was.

There was nothing for it but to return to the road, and attempt to get a lift to the docks. A small van, driven by a middle-aged Indian, braked to a halt in response to my signals. 'Kidderpore docks?' I asked without much hope, and to my surprise he nodded affably and opened the door to let me climb in.

The docks were a muddle of worn concrete, tall steel cranes, and groups of half-naked coolies. The hot air smelt of jute, oil and the rancid odour of the river. The ships were moored, stem to stern, lining the wharves in a long procession. They looked unutterably squalid and dirty, their decks festooned with hawsers, their gaping holds swallowing down sacks and wooden crates. I passed a dreary American tramp with the name *Homestead, Dallas* painted on its rusty stern, then the *Karagola*, the *West Pacific* and a large German boat with an unpronounceable name. Somehow I didn't like the sight of any of them much, and with the consoling thought that I had plenty of time to make up my mind, I crossed a bridge and found myself on another dock.

And here, lying in solitary splendour, white and spotless under the dazzling sunlight, was the ship of my dreams. A white ensign fluttered proudly from the mainmast. This small fighting ship, shining with fresh paint and gleaming brass, looked as attractive as a new toy, and yet every inch of its structure indicated that it was also a lethal instrument carefully designed for destruction. I walked from bow to stern, then back again. A narrow gangway led from the wharf to the lower deck, and at its head stood two sailors, apparently on guard, impeccable in their white tropical uniforms. As I watched this scene, a tall officer, wearing the stripes of a First Lieutenant, emerged from a hatch and approached the gangway. The two ratings stood aside to let him pass, and he walked briskly down the gangway on to the wharf. I thought at first that he was a young man, but a second look at his lean, rather weary face, told me that he was in his late thirties. He approached and stood beside me, and for a few seconds we stood in silence, looking towards the ship. Then he smiled and said affably, 'Well, what do you think of her?'

'I think she's wonderful,' I said with complete sincerity, and he smiled again, sharing my enthusiasm. Another pause ensued, then he asked off-handedly, 'Would you like to look her over?' I nodded gratefully, and the two of us climbed the gangplank onto the deck. I was to remember later that as we passed the two sailors, one of them looked knowingly towards his companion and seemed to wink.

I had learnt the hard way that life was full of unexpected dangers, and in ordinary circumstances I would certainly have thought twice before committing myself to an unknown man in unfamiliar surroundings. But in this case various complicated memories and convictions conspired to rob me of my usual caution. This was the Navy, the Royal Navy, and I had been brought up to believe that this was an institution above the frailties of ordinary mortals. Accordingly I followed my guide from one end of the ship to the other with childlike trust, fascinated and absorbed by all I saw.

Nobody was visible as we inspected the bridge and the gun turret, and wandered through numerous narrow steel passages. The officer chatted easily as we explored the intricate, sterile, inhuman interior of this fighting ship, and as I watched his thin, sensitive face I thought that I had seldom met a more likeable man. There was a point when I did feel a momentary unease, and that was when, towards the end of our tour, he led me deep into the bowels of the ship and approached an open hatch which seemed to lead to some ultimate abyss, close to the keel. We climbed down a steep, iron ladder and found ourselves in impenetrable darkness. I think he said that we were in the bilge, but the musty smell, the lack of headroom and the blackness suddenly got on my nerves. 'I don't much like this,' I said, and he answered immediately, 'All right, we'll go back on deck, and then if you like I'll show you my cabin.' In another minute we were back in the light, and I followed him into his small, bare cabin. He filled two glasses with lemonade, and joined me on the low divan that was obviously also used as his bunk.

We sat side by side, sipping the cold liquid and then, in a matter of seconds, a subtle change in his manner told me that something was wrong. He began to flatter me outrageously, but as he was certainly no actor, and approached this task with barely repressed distaste, his efforts to ingratiate himself with me rang as false as a cracked bell. Carefully avoiding my eyes, his face taut with guilty embarrassment, he continued doggedly on his self-imposed task. 'You know,' he told me insincerely, gazing fixedly at a point three feet above my head, 'You really are a most intelligent boy. I mean, you speak so well and seem to have travelled so widely that it's a real pleasure to talk to you.' His voice suddenly deepened. 'I'm sure,' he continued in a muffled whisper, 'You must have learnt to be fairly broad-minded about life, and realize that there's no harm in a bit of innocent fun.' As he rambled on, his long, sensitive hand, apparently acting of its own volition, fumbled its way towards my genitals. I slithered away from him, feeling not so much afraid, as sorry and embarrassed on his behalf. I was still sure that he was basically a decent, kindly man, and his clumsy efforts at seduction evoked a vague sense of pity for the humiliations he must have suffered in the attempt to satisfy his special needs. 'No,' I said, half apologetically, 'cut that out. I don't go in for that kind of stuff.' For the first time he lowered his eyes and looked at me directly. Immediately, his hand shot back, and his lips set in an angry line. 'Oh, come on,' he said irritably, 'don't be such a bloody prig,' but as I continued to resist his face darkened with disappointment and I instantly ceased to interest him. After that there seemed nothing more to say, so I rose awkwardly to my feet and moved towards the door. 'Thank you for showing me round,' I said with unnatural formality, but he didn't answer, and I hurried on deck and regained the wharf with a sensation of acute relief.

This encounter is only important because it extinguished my dreams of going to sea. What had happened was not very extraordinary, and yet just because it occurred at that particular time and place, I accepted it as an omen, warning me to keep my feet on land.

The evening was well advanced as I started to trudge back to the station. I did not attempt to thumb a lift, but about half a mile from the docks, a big green Wolseley drew into the curb and waited for me. An elderly Bengali woman, wearing a gorgeous yellow sari, stuck her head out of the window and asked whether I could direct her to Ballygunge. I did my best to oblige her, and during the brief conversation that ensued, managed to hint that I was bound in much the same direction and she instantly rose to the bait. 'I can take you as far as Sealdah,' she suggested cheerfully, and motioned me to climb inside the back seat.

When at last we reached Sealdah, I climbed out of the car with a sense of relief. By now the sun was low on the horizon and the city had reached a climax of noise and haste. Great crowds swarmed outside the station, while bullock carts, honking lorries and scampering rickshaws increased the confusion. I pushed my way through hordes of chattering Bengalis, tall, bearded Sikhs and plump, gold-turbaned Marwaris, and at last reached the platform. As I walked along it I half noticed a middle-aged man wearing some sort of uniform, moving towards me. I must have been very tired, because my brain failed to react to this signal of danger. The man passed me and though I was to remember later that he gazed at me intently, I ambled on without increasing my speed. I must have kept on for at least another ten or fifteen yards when, suddenly, a loud shout from behind me brought me to a standstill. 'I want a word with you.'

In another second the bulky, uniformed stranger was blocking my path. 'Your name is Greave and you're on the run from school. Don't waste your time trying to deny it; I've had a dozen telegrams giving me an exact description.' There didn't seem anything to say, so I kept silent. 'Come on,' he said brusquely, 'the sooner we get you to my office, the better it will be for all of us.' I followed him meekly to a small shabby office with the words Railway Police printed above its door.

For the next five hours I sat in that dark shoddy Police Office, trying not to listen to Inspector Collins' prolonged analysis of my colourful and varied crimes. But certain painful details were not to be evaded. I learnt, for example, that I had cost the school at least ten pounds in telegraphic fees alone, not to mention wasting the time of several dozen railway employees who had been searching trains and goods wagons. Inspector Collins had a gift for dramatic exposition, and by the time he was finished I was half convinced that the entire police force of Eastern Bengal, including tracker dogs, the detective branch and the narcotics squad, had dropped all their normal duties to ferret me out. With his close-cropped, greying hair and thick moustache, the Inspector looked every inch a policeman, but after a while, despite his hectoring voice, I realized that he was basically kind and understanding. After the initial explosion, his voice and manner became increasingly uncertain, until at last he said, in a voice that trembled with impotent irritation, 'You really are a bloody nuisance. I don't want to send you back with an Indian constable, but I don't see what else I can do.'

'I'm sorry,' I murmured feebly, and at this he snorted, 'Sorry! Sorry! What good is being sorry to me?' 'Well,' I began weakly, 'it really was a horrible school and they used to beat you with . . .' but he cut me short. 'Beat you, did they? Well you probably needed beating. Anyway, my business is to return you where you belong.' And then he seemed to melt suddenly, because he said almost sympathetically, 'I suppose you haven't had a square meal for days,' and without waiting for an answer, sent one of his men out to bring me a large tea from the refreshment room.

As I ate hungrily, trying to forget that he was there, I could hear him fussing and fuming on the other side of the desk. When I finished eating, we sat looking at each other in silence, and then suddenly he smiled, leaned forward, and tapped my shoulder appeasingly. 'Now, look here,' he said, 'I'm sure you don't want to cause us a lot of unnecessary trouble, so I'm going to trust you, and give you a chance to make it the easy way.' Still smiling, he paused dramatically. 'Just give me your word, your word of honour, that you'll go back on your own, and I'll buy you a ticket and you can walk out of this office any time you like.' I hesitated for a moment, because I really hated having to disappoint him, but I knew that it was quite impossible for me to do as he asked. I just couldn't have lived with myself had I surrendered so tamely. 'No,' I said, 'I couldn't give you my word. I'd make a run for it the first chance I got.'

He half rose from his chair, his leathery yellow face turning a bright red. 'You blasted young fool,' he bellowed, 'give me any more cheek and I'll send you back in handcuffs.' I said nothing, and after a minute he got out of his chair and lurched towards the door, murmuring more to himself than to me, 'I've got to arrange something. There must be some way of getting rid of this bastard.' I heard a click, and a little later he was telephoning somebody, and this process was repeated several times.

I sat staring at a kind of rack on the wall containing an assortment of sinister handcuffs and leg-irons, and succumbed to a mood of deep melancholy. A very long hour dragged by, and then I heard the loud, purposeful thud of the Inspector's footsteps. He was smiling broadly. He opened a drawer, extracted a large cigar, stuck it between his lips, leaned back and gazed at me triumphantly. 'Well, my boy,' he said jovially, 'it's all worked out, and whether you like it or not, you'll be back in that bloody school in less than twenty-four hours.'

It appeared that one of our senior boys, a tall, gangly creature named Carl whom I particularly detested, had been compelled to leave the school temporarily and return to Calcutta because of some unspecified family complications. 'We've had a talk,' continued the Inspector, puffing happily away at his cigar, 'and he's agreed to look after you and take good care you don't do anything silly on the way back.'

The prospect of being escorted to that hateful school in the custody of this self-righteous youth was almost more than I could bear. Unfortunately, he was so much older and larger than myself that the idea of using force to get away from him was simply not realistic. I remained sullenly silent as I sought to prepare myself for what lay ahead.

Thirty minutes before the Mail was due to leave, I heard Carl's hateful, high-pitched voice in the next room, and a second later the door opened and in he came, cold blue eyes glinting behind his glasses, radiating self-satisfaction. We looked at each other with mutual distaste, and while his teeth were bared in an unctuous smile, my face merely expressed the stoicism of a victim on his way to the rack. 'So here you are, young Greave,' he said. 'I'm sorry to hear you've been giving everybody a lot of trouble.' He turned to the Inspector and continued patronizingly, 'He always was a young bastard, sir, but don't you worry, I'll see that he gets back to school if I have to break his arm.' 'No need for that,' said the Inspector virtuously, and for some time the two of them discussed me with a candour that I found extremely galling. At last my warder rose to his feet, walked towards me and gripped my arm with long bony fingers. 'We'd better be going,' he said courteously to the Inspector, and turning his head and lowering his voice, he whispered in my ear, 'Don't try any tricks, or I'll just have to beat you up.' In this fashion, defeated and a prisoner, I boarded the train and prepared to retrace my journey towards captivity.

We were now travelling second class, and the compartment was empty except for a Bengali clerk. Carl hovered round me every minute, even following me when I went to the lavatory, and it soon became clear that he proposed to make the most of his brief authority. I had to listen to another long lecture, in addition to several sinister prophecies describing what was likely to happen to me immediately I was handed over to the Brothers. Finally my patience broke. 'Can't you shut up, you silly bastard? Don't you think I'm in enough trouble without having to listen to your hypocritical whining?' After that, he gave up speaking to me directly, and turning to the Indian clerk, compelled him to listen to a detailed recital of my errors. He discussed my imperfections as though I were some kind of inanimate object, talking about me over my head, while the two of them looked at me with the detached fascinated horror usually reserved for a freak at a side-show. And as he piled it on, the Indian nodded and clicked his tongue sympathetically, murmuring 'Is that so indeed? He must be a pukka villain. What reprehensible goings-on,' until the cup of my humiliation was filled to the brim.

After about half an hour of this, I rose to my feet, saying shortly, 'I want to go to sleep.' Carl pointed to one of the upper bunks, and I obediently climbed into it, turned my back on an unsympathetic world, and tried to forget my miseries. I must have been dead tired, because in a matter of seconds I fell into a deep sleep.

The train plunged on through the darkness, and when I awoke the compartment was dark and silent. I peered out of the small window close to my head, and saw that we had come to a halt at a small wayside station. A tiny platform lay below me. Not a single human was visible, though some distance away flickering light suggested some sort of activity. The air smelt fresh and cool. It must have been long past midnight. I pulled myself up on my elbow, craned my neck, and looked down into the compartment. Carl was lying on his stomach, his head turned at an angle, snoring with rhythmic precision, and the plump Indian, hands folded on his chest, was also engulfed in the depths of sleep. Moving with infinite care, I slid from the upper berth to the floor. I paused, took another look at the two slumbering figures, and then began to move, an inch at a time, towards the door that opened on the side opposite to the platform. Doors on Indian railways are heavy and cumbersome, and I dreaded the rasping scrape it was likely to make when I attempted to drag it open. But my luck was in, and the handle slipped down without a sound.

I stumbled, and fell forward on my hands as I hit the rough path below the door. Scrambling to my feet, I noticed that I had cut the palm of my right hand on the sharp gravel. I started to walk silently, but as rapidly as possible, past the long line of coaches towards the rear of the train. My immediate objective was to find somewhere to hide. I could not guess how long it would be before Carl awoke and noticed my absence, and if the alarm was raised during the next few minutes, my hopes of avoiding detection on this lonely station would be slim indeed. I prayed desperately for the train to start and leave me in peace, but the wheels remained motionless, and it seemed a long, long, time before I passed the last coach.

I looked to my right and saw nothing but the empty platform. To my left was a flat expanse of withered grass without enough cover to conceal a rabbit. No hiding place there. At any moment I expected to hear the clamour of voices and the clatter of feet running after me. And then, between the railway lines, I saw what looked like a long, narrow ditch about four feet deep, and ten yards in length. I discovered later that this queer trough was known as a cleaning pit, and that its purpose was to allow maintenance men to get under a standing coach and carry out inspection and repairs; but at that time it simply represented an answer to my problem, and I scrambled down and crouched inside it. Peering over the top, I could clearly see the red light at the end of the train about thirty yards ahead. I seemed to remain in that smelly pit for at least half an hour, but I suppose that in fact it could not have been more than seven or eight minutes. At last, to my unutterable relief, a whistle shrieked, the train jerked, and I watched the red light gradually disappear into the night.

10

My escape was a moment of real triumph. I found myself chuckling as I pictured Carl's expression when he awoke to find that I had given him the slip. The station platform, blurred by night, was like a ghost town. Every door and window was locked tight, and the only refuge I could find for the rest of the night was a dilapidated wooden bench. I passed an extremely uncomfortable night, and whenever I succeeded in falling into a doze, the sounds made by some sort of animal – I took it to be a pariah dog – scuffling and rooting about the platform, jerked me awake. I vaguely remember shouting at the beast, and once I flung a stone in the direction of the sound. But at last the dawn came, and I passed into a deep sleep.

When I awoke, blinking in the dazzling sunlight, the platform was alive with noise and movement. The station-master's office was open, but was so crowded that it was not easy to force an entrance. The small space was filled with Indians, mostly peasants from the local farms, who obviously used it as a convenient meeting place. Some of them, squatting on the floor, grasped baskets laden with fruit and vegetables, others clutched half a dozen live chickens, and I noticed a large white goat standing with aloof dignity on the counter, hemmed in by gesticulating humans. The focal point of the scene was the placid, corpulent, station-master, standing in comparative isolation behind his untidy desk. Everybody looked up in amazement as I made my entrance, and I got the impression that strangers were hardly ever seen at this primitive, lonely station. The locals clustered round me, curious but helpful. I was mortified to hear that the only train likely to be of the least use to me was not due to arrive till late that evening. 'Most of the fast trains do not stop here,' explained the station-master cheerfully. He was chewing *pan* energetically, and paused every few seconds to discharge a mass of red spittle on the floor. Just to say something, I mentioned my experience during the night. 'I wish you'd chase that damn dog off your platform,' I said. 'It made such a row I couldn't get to sleep.' The station-master looked at me in silence, and then began to laugh uncontrollably. 'That was no dog, sir,' he spluttered. 'There are no dogs on this station. What you heard was a panther, sir. It comes every night, and therefore we are compelled to keep the waiting room closed up.' He then explained what had happened to the others, who all treated it as a great joke.

I had stumbled across the real India. These people lived in a way that had hardly changed in a thousand years, and they possessed a kind of innocence and simplicity totally unlike the suspicion and distrust displayed by the denizens of the city. They knew nothing of politics, and because their lives were involved with the great, natural processes of the earth, there was a tranquillity, a lack of haste, in all they did.

I was touched and astonished by their efforts to help me. They insisted on offering me a chair behind the station-master's desk, and within a few minutes I was dining sumptuously on chapatties, curry and a glass of steaming tea. After that, a young man, the son of one of the village elders, more or less adopted me. He was about five years older than me, immensely proud of his ability to speak English, and we seemed to take to each other on sight. He led me past clumps of bamboo, across paddy fields to the small village which was his home. I heard that his heart was set on getting to Calcutta, enrolling at the University, and studying for his BA degree. His eyes glowed with enthusiasm as he described this ambition, and I could tell that he was convinced that the magic letters 'BA' after his name would instantly transport him to an enchanted world. Followed by hordes of small children, we entered his home, where I was introduced to his father, a bearded patriarch, and was soon accepted as one of the family. The women, shielding their faces coyly with the folds of their saris, peered at us curiously, but never approached except for some domestic purpose. Their hospitality was lavish, and though I had just eaten, half a dozen enormous mangoes were produced and I realized that it would have caused offence to refuse them. The old man's English was rudimentary but, using his son as an interpreter, he discussed the perils of life in Calcutta, listening to my opinions with touching faith.

I really enjoyed the next few hours. We explored the village and finally cooled our sweat-stained bodies by a swim in a large, green pool. When evening came, I was escorted back to the station, forced to accept a generous assortment of greasy Indian sweets, and put aboard the waiting train. The old man and his son stood on the platform and waved farewell.

Thirty-six hours later, exhausted and hungry, I alighted at Galundo railway station. Galundo was a particularly large and dirty station, close to the turgid waters of the Ganges. This part of the country was dominated by the river, and at times it was difficult to recognize the dividing line between the water and the dry land. The enormous river seemed perpetually on the point of overwhelming the low-lying sodden earth. Hundreds of boats, squat and clumsy, jammed close together a few feet from the shore, formed a floating town, and the air smelt of mud and water. This was as far as the railway went, and I could only continue my journey by boarding a river steamer to Chandpore, from where the Assam Mail steamed towards the frontier. By now my capital had been reduced to the equivalent of five pence, so that I was in no position to pay for a proper meal.

The people here seemed smaller and darker than the inhabitants of Central Bengal, but their lack of stature did nothing to diminish the strength of their voices, and as I pushed through the crowd, the noise was deafening. Eventually I reached the wharf and surveyed the craft on which I hoped to cover the next stage of my journey. I saw a large, flat-bottomed paddle steamer with a high superstructure and two long, narrow black funnels set side by side. It looked exactly like pictures I had seen of the river boats on the Mississippi, and was probably built to a similar design. A gangway reached from the ship to the jetty, but its lower end was guarded by some sort of official who was carefully inspecting each passenger's ticket. I watched him for about a quarter of an hour, but he showed no sign of leaving his post for a single second.

Then I saw a young Indian girl, shy and graceful, her black hair woven into a long plait, emerge from the crowd. As I watched her, she came to a halt, and stood glancing uncertainly round her. The man who was guarding the gangway, turned his head and caught sight of her. His face lightened, and he called out to her, but because of the noisy crowd that streamed between them the girl did not hear. The man called again, and then swung round and hurried towards her. That was all I needed. Within fifteen seconds I had crossed the gangway and gained the comparative safety of the upper deck. In another moment, I had found an empty cabin and darted inside, locking the door behind me.

As I sat on the bunk, a variety of crashes and shouts told me that we were on the point of departure. The floor under my feet tilted slightly and then the great paddles began to revolve. When I left my cabin the shore had receded and we were steaming across the vast surface of the Ganges.

The lower deck was crowded with a vociferous horde of poor Indians. They stood, crouched or sat, on every available inch of space, guarding large baskets filled with rice and vegetables, or clutching hold of goats and sheep. In contrast, the first-class quarters on the upper deck were almost empty, apart from a tall European who stood at the rails, staring with aloof distaste across the water. His name, Lieutenant-Colonel Cox-Harrison, was inscribed in bold lettering on a couple of expensive suitcases. Probably he was off on a shooting holiday in the jungles of Assam.

There must have been other passengers lurking somewhere, but if so, I did not see them. After a while, I found myself peering into the saloon. A long table, gleaming with cutlery and glass, lay waiting in opulent confidence for those passengers capable of paying for an expensive lunch. I stared at it with ravenous fascination, hoping to detect some fragments of real food amongst all this glittering splendour. All that was visible was an enormous bunch of yellow bananas in the centre of the table. Not a waiter, not a deckhand was in sight. I slipped quickly through the open door, seized the bananas and ran back to my cabin. Sitting on the floor, I disposed of thirteen succulent bananas in the space of rather less than two minutes. As each one disappeared, I flung the empty skin on the floor beside me, and I still remember, before I was half-way through my meal, observing a long line of hungry ants marching out of the woodwork to claim their share of the feast.

A quarter of an hour later, I was nabbed yet again. By now this procedure had become so familiar that I hardly bothered to portray outraged astonishment and innocence, but merely accepted the inevitable. This time, after a prolonged wrangle with one of the ship's officers, I was finally summoned to the bridge where the captain was waiting to see me. Two Lascars escorted me up various narrow stairs until at last I found myself in the awe-inspiring presence of the skipper. He was so completely unlike my mental image of a ship's captain that at first I could only stare at him. He was a small, wiry, oldish man, with a scraggy red beard, bloodshot blue eyes, and a shiny bald pate. He was wearing a crumpled pyjama jacket and blue serge trousers, and his feet were encased in battered bedroom slippers. He was lying back in a deck chair, clutching a bottle of Johnnie Walker when I appeared, but immediately he saw me he got to his feet, placed the bottle on the floor, picked up his peaked nautical cap, put it on his head, and glared at me ferociously.

In a voice slurred by whisky and a rich brogue, he opened the conversation by snarling, 'What the hell do you mean by stowing away on this ship, you bloody young whippersnapper?' I tried to say something but was instantly interrupted by a savage bellow. 'None of your bloody lies.' For the next five minutes he ranted on, and at last, panting slightly, he suddenly lowered his voice and said, 'Well, my boyo, you're not getting away with this. I'm going to hand you over to the Railway Police the moment we dock. They'll know how to treat an impudent young bastard who's probably run away from a good Catholic school.' I could think of nothing to say, and after some moments of embarrassed silence, he returned to his seat, and I was allowed back to my original quarters.

I hadn't the faintest idea of what I was going to do when we reached Chandpore, but the knowledge that this problem need not be faced for several hours revived my natural optimism, and I settled down to make the most of my brief immunity. I bought ten of the cheapest bazaar cigarettes from one of the Lascars; I remember that they were called 'Polo' and that they tasted like old straw. Puffing happily on one of these loathsome cigarettes, I stationed myself on the rails close to the tall military individual and tried to start a conversation. But he refused to respond to my overtures, which were brought to an ignoble conclusion when he suddenly rasped, 'For heaven's sake, leave me alone and stop suffocating me with that filthy cigarette.' Looking at me with marked distaste, he then pointedly moved down the rails.

Every hour or so, the steamer would draw into some tiny islet or waterlogged shoreline and disembark scores of passengers, who were immediately replaced by others. The ship was constructed in such a way that it could approach within a few feet of the sodden shore, allowing the passengers to wade through the muddy waters and clamber aboard the lower decks.

This was a strange, sinister country. The waterlogged land, flat and treeless, stretched away as far as the eye could reach. Squalid, mis-shapen villages crouched like animals about to be engulfed by the greedy waters of the river. The people, small, dark and half naked, seemed to be engaged in an endless battle against the hostile forces of nature. I got the impression that to survive here one had to possess the strength and tenacity of a jungle creature, yet the crowds that gathered to meet the boat flashed their white teeth in boisterous laughter, and joked and gossiped with irrepressible good humour. I still had two bananas, all that was left of my original stock. Out of a mixture of fun and pity, I flung one of these at a youth of about my own age who stood knee-deep in the shallows, staring up at me from the shore. He caught it with a swift movement of his hand, and after a moment, entering into the spirit of the game, chucked a small mango towards me. Unfortunately, his aim was not particularly accurate, and the pulpy fruit struck the rails within a couple of inches of my unfriendly military companion. He turned on me furiously. 'Can't you stop worrying those bloody natives?'

Night was falling as the sparkle of distant lights warned me that we were approaching Chandpore. Now fear and uncertainty returned. In one way or another, it was absolutely essential for me to get off that boat before the captain had time to hand me over. I climbed down to the lower deck, pushing my way through the crowd until I reached the point where I thought the gangway would probably be lowered. If I could make a dash for it the instant it fell into place, there was just a chance of reaching the wharf and getting away. The roar of the paddle wheels ceased as we drifted the last few yards towards the dock. The gangs of Lascars heaved ropes over the side, and a moment later the gangway swung forward and hit the wharf with a crash. I leapt forward, determined to be the first to cross it, and then slowed to a despairing halt. My luck was out. A uniformed official had already stationed himself beside the gangway.

The Indian passengers began to hurry ashore, and with a sinking heart I watched him check each ticket with scrupulous care. I stood wondering how long it would be before the captain, or one of his emissaries, appeared to take me in charge. Anything was better than waiting, and I moved forward with the crowd and started my perilous journey down the gangway. I moved as slowly as I could, but the people behind jostled me forward, and at last I heard the sinister words, 'Your ticket, please?' I hesitated, craning my head backwards in an effort to gain a few extra seconds, and there, just a dozen feet behind me, I saw Lieutenant-Colonel Cox-Harrison, followed by two coolies bearing his luggage, picking his way delicately towards the shore.

Inspiration suddenly cleared my muddled brain. I turned my head and looked straight into the ticket collector's face. 'My father has the tickets,' I said, gesturing with my thumb towards the Colonel. The man waved me past, and in another moment I was lost in the crowd. I sometimes wonder what the Colonel said when he discovered that he had been presented with an unwanted son.

A hundred yards beyond the wharf lay Chandpore Railway Station. The platform extended a long, long way, and the fact that it appeared completely empty, except for my solitary figure, was extremely unnerving: I felt oddly unreal as I moved forward under the glare of the lights. I half thought that perhaps I had died somewhere on the boat and was now condemned to wander endlessly through a sort of limbo from which there was no escape. And then I saw an empty train waiting beside the platform. The long line of carriages was in darkness and there was no locomotive steaming and puffing at its head. The figure of a stout Anglo-Indian woman wearing a peaked cap, and something that looked vaguely like a uniform, emerged from the shadows. When she was within a yard of me, I planted myself in her path and for a moment or two we inspected each other without a word. 'Is this the Assam Mail?' I asked, and when she nodded I blurted out, 'Where's the engine? What's it doing standing there like a ghost train?' She looked at me pityingly. 'It is not due to depart for another three hours,' she said pedantically, 'and the lights and the engine will all turn up in due course.'

This was bad news indeed. For some reason, I had never doubted that the Mail was likely to leave within minutes of the boat's arrival. I touched depths of fear and uncertainty during the course of the next few hours that were far worse than anything I had experienced before. The Railway Police were probably looking for me even now, and where could I find cover on this long, empty, brilliantly illuminated platform? In the end, I found a small, dark coupé, clearly marked 'Reserved for Females', and scrambled inside. Each window was tightly shut, and with the certainty that I was totally invisible from the platform, I sat down on one of the padded berths.

The next three hours passed like a nightmare. Gradually the platform became increasingly crowded and every minute or two something happened that convinced me that my luck had finally run out. Strange voices rose and fell just outside my window, once somebody half-opened the door, then decided to close it again. A sudden jerk and a loud hissing of steam, as the locomotive attached itself to the train, was so unexpected that my heart seemed literally to lunge into my throat. A dozen hours seemed to elapse, and then I heard the sound of rapidly approaching footsteps accompanied by hoarse male laughter. I jumped up and pushed my way into the dark toilet, closing the door behind me. A cheerful voice boomed in rich chee chee, 'What the hell, the bastard must be miles away by now. Let's go and have a drink.' Another voice appeared to disagree, and then the first speaker bellowed on a note of jovial resignation, 'All right, just this last one, but I tell you the bugger couldn't be on this train.' Standing in the darkness I held my breath and actually prayed. The door opened with a thud, heavy boots clattered on the floor. At one point they must have been within six inches of my shrinking body. The first voice proclaimed, 'There you are, I told you so, let's go and get ourselves that drink.' The footsteps retreated, the door closed with a bang.

Now, for some inexplicable reason, I was certain that everything was going to be all right. An instinct, strong and reliable, told me that my luck was in. A minute later the lights flashed on, and I sat blinking owlishly. Gongs sounded, the train shuddered and began to move. After a little while, I opened the window and cautiously looked outside. By now the train had gathered speed and was plunging into the hot darkness at sixty or seventy miles an hour. I sat there watching the mysterious Indian countryside, encased in darkness, flash past the train, and for a short time experienced a sensation of perfect happiness. I was never to forget the next few minutes, and they were to remain in my mind as moments of shining magnificence. The fact that I had at last achieved my objective and was now so close to Silchar that nobody would take the trouble to turn me back, was supremely satisfying. As the train sped through the night, I sat staring into the darkness, savouring my fragment of heaven.

When I awoke, the train was drawing into Silchar. It was a bright, clear morning as I stepped out onto the platform and started on the last stage of my long journey. They were checking tickets at the barrier, so I simply turned round and kept walking in the opposite direction until the platform ended and I was able to leave the station without detection. It was easy enough to learn that the Spragues' bungalow was about four miles away, down a narrow muddy track that led through thick scrub. I managed the first three miles fairly well, and then suddenly extreme fatigue broke over me. The path wound between a series of small rounded hillocks covered in thick jungle. At last I came to a large pool, very still and deep, under the shadow of a much bigger hill. I skirted its base and came in sight of a bungalow with a thatched roof. The path sloped up towards it, and by now I was so tired that I could barely force my legs to move. I saw that there were two coolies squatting on the roof of the bungalow, apparently repairing its thatch, and as I drew closer they both raised their heads and looked at me. And then, quite suddenly something happened to the bungalow, the coolies, and the clear blue sky. They all seemed to fall together, swaying and plunging as they slipped out of perspective. The ground came rushing up to meet me and I realized that I had fallen on the muddy path. I seem to remember loud cries from the two coolies, who were now scrambling towards the ground, and then I came to a dark nothingness.

When I recovered consciousness I was inside the house, lying on a couch, and Mrs Sprague and an Indian servant were bending over me, their eyes full of solicitude. After that everything went much better than I had planned. Mrs Sprague listened to my story with sympathetic understanding, and assured me that I could stay with her as long as I liked. She wrote to Bombay explaining what had happened, and soon received a reply from my mother assuring her that she was only too glad to leave me in Assam until the end of term.

The months which followed brought me almost perfect happiness. In these primitive surroundings the days slipped past in leisurely content. For the first time since I had left Calcutta I was conscious of being completely free, and everything around me was strange and wonderful. I was soon able to accept the silent bungalow with its high, airy rooms as a real home.

The jungle was very close, and the veranda was screened from the world outside by wire netting to discourage snakes and other wild creatures from paying impromptu visits. Directly in front of the bungalow, perhaps six or seven hundred yards away, was another, much larger hill, thickly overgrown with trees and bushes, which was occupied by a community of Hindu monks.

We could just see the roofs of half a dozen huts, partially concealed by the dense foliage, but in every other respect they were so unobtrusive and retiring that we were barely conscious of their existence. Once or twice, when I was skirting the deep, silent pool I had passed when I first came, I would see a solitary figure, clad in a long saffron robe, slipping like a ghost between the trees; but their rapid retreat from such encounters clearly showed that they had no desire for intimacy. The only other evidence of their presence was the muted sound of a gong which drifted towards us soon after noon and in the late evening, but this recurring ritual soon became so familiar that we ceased to notice it. Flocks of wild geese would alight on the surface of that mysterious pond, and the monks apparently welcomed their presence, because food would be left for them.

Mr Sprague was short but stocky, with a lined, weatherbeaten face and thinning hair. His grey eyes peered at the world with patient, watchful resignation. He was employed as a driller by one of the large British oil companies, and though his education was almost negligible, his knowledge and experience in the art of sinking a well brought him a very good salary. In those days, English drillers simply did not exist and it was necessary to recruit them from the United States on extremely liberal terms. I soon grew really fond of the simplicity and innate kindliness of this slow-spoken, gentle character. He had been born in Ohio in extreme poverty and as a young man had drifted west to work as a cow-puncher on an enormous ranch. When we were alone, I would listen with complete absorption to his stories of the hard-riding, hard-living men who earned their living on the open range.

On another low ridge, about three hundred yards from the bungalow, stood the tall wooden derrick which straddled the oil well Sprague was attempting to bore. The base of this structure, smelling of oil, grease and sweat, housed the complicated drilling gear which was gradually sinking deeper and deeper into the earth. If my memory is reliable, he had reached a depth of over a thousand feet when I first came to Assam. Every now and then, the drill, a long shaft of metal perhaps eight feet long and as thick as a man's waist, would be dragged to the surface to be changed or repaired. This grey, metal shaft seemed oddly formidable and a little terrifying as it emerged from the narrow, deep hole down which it had burrowed so effectively. The digging end of the shaft would be smeared with a rich deposit of blue shale, as soft as butter and as delicately tinted as a flower. Sprague would stretch out his arm and collect a handful of this mysterious, liquid mud. He would sniff the stuff delicately, and I gathered that a real driller could smell oil long before the biting end of the shaft had found it. Sprague was confident that his drills were very close to the black riches which lay concealed somewhere deep underground.

A gang of about twelve coolies worked with him at the well. Gaunt and half naked, their brown skins glistening with sweat, they seemed to enjoy their work, and I know that they considered Sprague to be a just and undemanding boss. He would joke with them in his broken Hindi and prompt them to harmless horse-play, during which one of them would seize the hose and direct a long stream of water at his laughing companions. I visited the well every day, often remaining there for several hours, and in time I learned enough about the business to appreciate some of its more subtle, exciting possibilities. Sinking a well was like playing the horses; sometimes one was lucky enough to choose a winner, but more often months and even years of sustained effort drew a blank. Sprague had the reputation of a lucky driller, and the deeper the shaft penetrated the more feverish became his suspense when the oil still refused to be found.

I spent about six months in that small, lonely bungalow, a time of almost flawless happiness. I was free, there was the jungle, and the special intricate world of the oil wells to explore. As I remember it, the sun shone every day, and in the cool of the evening a wind sighed gently through the trees, and wild Paddy birds drifted slowly across the sky. For my birthday the Spragues presented me with an air rifle. This weapon, with its long black barrel and perfectly modelled stock, brought me closer to heaven than almost anything I was to experience in the future. For several weeks after it had been given to me, I would wake up very early and walk across the rice fields which fringed the jungle. The air smelt sweet and clean, and wisps of mist still floated above the trees and bushes. This was my private world, and I could wander through it for hours without seeing another human. I would shoot at snipe, jackals, and the small green parrots which flashed across the sky. I can't remember killing anything, but that did nothing to spoil the fun. I didn't think of it like this then, of course, but those dawn wanderings probably achieved a pinnacle of happiness that I would never find again. For me, at least, a boy, a gun and the jungle, were the ingredients of perfection. Once I saw two wolves, loping away towards cover, and actually took a shot at them with my absurd rifle.

When I was not wandering or dreaming, I read for hours at a stretch. The Spragues' library was not extensive, consisting as it did of a single open book-case on which thirty or forty books were neatly arranged. They were an odd collection, ranging from Zane Grey through Conrad to the short stories of de Maupassant. I read them all, not once but several times, and through their pages glimpsed a hundred fantastic, undiscovered worlds.

My life in Assam was necessarily lonely, and yet I can never remember feeling either bored or isolated. Each day produced something unusual or exciting. One evening I saw a tiger vanishing through the tall grass bordering the rough track that led to the bungalow. I say I saw a tiger, but in fact all I saw was a vivid flash of gold and black disappearing through the foliage.

Every Saturday a battered taxi carried us into the town of Silchar for our weekly shopping. As I recall it, we always went to the same, large untidy shop which was generally crowded with other drillers and tea planters. This establishment was presided over by a suave gentleman named Mr Munday, and appeared to sell everyhing from a reel of cotton to a double-barrelled shotgun. I was enchanted by the diversity of its wares, much of it bought in bulk from planters disposing of all their possessions before returning to England. The dusty shelves were crammed with old novels, riding boots, chipped teapots, brandy glasses and boxes of rifle ammunition. I would spend hours wandering from one large, untidy room to another. Once I went with Mrs Sprague to the planters' yearly gymkhana and spent the entire afternoon and evening skirting tents and ponies, while the planting fraternity, most of them drunk, indulged in a series of races and mock battles, which would have made a Western rodeo seem as peaceful as a kindergarten. Sprague would often take me shooting, and we would board dug-out canoes and paddle through the yellow, weed-infested waters of the rivers which abounded in that district. Wild duck and snipe were plentiful, and we would often return with twenty or thirty duck and as many snipe. Sprague harboured the secret dream of bagging a tiger, but though he often followed the trail of these creatures, he never did succeed in getting one.

From a boy's point of view, it was all pure magic. Even now the memory of those months in the wilderness remains intact and beautiful, one of the few fragments from my childhood undisturbed by either anxiety or guilt.

II

After those unforgettable months in Assam, I rejoined my family in Bombay. My brother had returned home for the school holidays and I found them installed in a large flat, four storeys above the crowded street, overlooking a small dreary park ornamented by unkempt bushes and several rusty benches. This part of the city was then known as Elphinstone Circle, and below, to the left of our long veranda, we could see a pretentious edifice that had once been Bombay's Town Hall. Far behind this building, green as jade and glittering under the fierce sunlight, the harbour was just visible.

My homecoming was quite original: in some extraordinary fashion, I managed to fall down the lift shaft on the lower floor, and presented myself to my family in a somewhat dishevelled condition, with a face richly smeared with thick, black oil. I learnt that my father had started an advertising agency; probably the first of its kind to appear in India, and that his office consisted of a single, enormous room adjoining our private quarters. In these surroundings, my father's few careworn, harassed employees – a couple of Goanese artists, an embittered stenographer, and several Indian clerks – worked at feverish speed, hemmed in by untidy filing cabinets, half-finished posters and the like. My father's voice, loud and menacing, could frequently be heard, exhorting these unfortunates to fresh efforts. But most of his energy was expended in plunging about the city in search of business, from which forays he returned streaming with sweat, and in the worst of tempers. Surprisingly enough, this enterprise soon achieved considerable success, and with fresh orders pouring in every day, he was soon earning a comfortable living. However, only a very small part of these profits reached his family, and none of us could guess how he spent the rest of them.

He must have been nearly forty by then, but his appearance had hardly changed. His hair was still jet black, his back straight, and he had lost none of his aggressive confidence. But my mother, though she was still astonishingly beautiful, had not escaped so lightly. She was still cheerful and tranquil, but something that had once been radiant and hopeful had left her face forever. She must have realized by now that she was involved in a struggle that could only end in defeat. She had entrusted her life to a man who could not help but destroy everything he touched. She must, long since, have accepted the bitter fact that her dreams – a small house, a cherished garden, and normal security – must forever remain out of reach. Nevertheless, she strove yet again to create a home in these unpromising surroundings; and indeed, as she had done so often before, she did succeed in establishing some kind of order, a measure of security, in the face of difficulties that might well have been considered insurmountable. At least she had her children under one roof, and with her usual dedicated, unselfish concentration, she tried yet again to create a home for all of us.

My sister Mary, now a pretty, intelligent child of nearly six, had returned to us after an absence of over a year in the custody of Miss Felloni. She had long fair plaits, and an engaging smile, but her personality displayed qualities of timidity and submission that had certainly not been apparent before. The influence of Miss F, a lonely Edwardian spinster with an instinctive distaste for childish exuberance, had transformed our small wild-cat into a pampered, self-righteous prig. But the rowdy, nomadic habits of her long-lost family soon succeeded in extinguishing these objectionable traits. Within a few weeks, the artificially imposed inhibitions had almost completely vanished, to be replaced by the tough, resilient, talkative character I had once known so well. Again I became her chief ally and friend, defending her against my brother's irritability, and mother's well-meaning efforts to discipline a personality which resisted the slightest hint of coercion. I loved her very much, and in those early years a bond of understanding and sympathy was forged between us which was to survive the passage of time and change. She was an impulsive, warm-hearted child, quite exceptionally intelligent and perceptive, and her capacity for generosity and fun was almost unlimited. Even in those days she was constantly immersed in a book, and as her tastes were completely unsupervised, she absorbed a wide range of literature that most people would have considered completely unsuitable for a young child. Like most elder brothers, I tormented her unmercifully, but nothing I did permanently changed our mutual affection.

Bombay in the 1920s was a colourful and exciting city. It was crowded and noisy, but its narrow, twisting lanes throbbed with life and vitality. Because it was surrounded on three sides by the sea, one could never get far away from the harbour, the docks, or the long line of its golden beaches. The city was bursting with colour and energy, cosmopolitan and enterprising, and yet somehow completely Indian. I spent every available hour close to the sea. I would watch the old, ponderous dhows from Zanzibar, discharging their cargo. They were owned by Arabs, who had sailed for centuries between Africa and India. Nobody understood how they managed to find their way across thousands of miles of ocean without even the simplest navigational instruments, but some kind of instinct guided them to their haven, and the green waters of the harbour were seldom free of their triangular, primitive sails.

My father started a monthly magazine named *The Sportsman*. Despite the fact that something like seventy-five per cent of the population of India were totally illiterate, he was convinced that there were millions of people longing to read such a publication. My mother, reluctant and suspicious, was compelled to undertake the task of writing the women's page. She had no confidence in her ability as a journalist, but I think now that her contributions were probably the only worthwhile part of the magazine. My father was absolutely convinced that this paper would soon achieve a circulation of half a million. He pointed out that everybody in India was interested in tigers, and succeeded in inducing several well-known hunters to describe their experiences in long, boring articles. He never offered to pay for these contributions, and to the best of my knowledge was never asked to do so. This magazine engrossed all his attention for several months. I can still remember its bilious, yellow cover, with the words, 'Editor, H. Greave' printed in bold, black lettering. But after a while it must have become increasingly difficult to discover obliging tiger killers, and eventually, after about six months, *The Sportsman* passed away with the minimum of publicity.

I hung around the Marine docks, although they were technically out of bounds to unauthorized civilians, for hundreds of hours. Each one of these regions possessed its special attractions, though, of course, they were all in close proximity to the sea and ships. Ballards Pier, for example, was the point from which, every Friday, the weekly P & O mail boat sailed for England. This ritual never failed to produce scenes of excitement and drama, and I would stand inconspicuously among the crowd, utterly engrossed until the last hawser was cast off, and the great screws began to revolve, beating the water into a seething mass of green and white. In those days the abbreviation 'P & O' conjured up a kind of magic, and the lean, sombre ships, black-hulled, their superstructure painted a sickly yellow, were a guarantee that somewhere, far beyond the limits of the horizon, the homeland did, in fact, exist.

Some of the ships I saw then – I am thinking particularly of the gallant *Rawalpindi* – were destined to achieve tragic fame years later. But none of us could have guessed in those years that this great ship, graceful and apparently invulnerable in the hot, Indian sunlight, would meet its death in the cold, grey Atlantic, battered by German guns.

At other times, I would swim for hours in the shabby bath on Back Bay Beach, or explore mysterious creeks where the dhows unloaded their cargo, surrounded by scores of sweating, almost naked coolies. The sea, and the city, were a boy's paradise, and I was never bored during my prolonged explorations of both. Apart from the few, wretched hours I spent in class, I was completely free with an entire world waiting to be explored.

For the next nine months my life contained little except bright sunlight and green sea. I had no real objective except to dream and explore, and these activities satisfied me completely. And then, both my brother and I contracted malaria. Two or three times a week, generally towards the late evening, our temperature soared, violent ague followed, and finally delirium took over. We lost weight rapidly, and our faces became pinched and yellow. We absorbed enormous doses of quinine, then the only treatment available, but our health continued to deteriorate. Eventually, my father decided that it was essential to get us out of Bombay, and my mother suggested a tiny hamlet high up on the Western Ghats named Panchgani. I think now that father had become profoundly bored with his unfortunate family and that his apparent kindness masked an urgent desire to be rid of us.

In less than a week, my mother and we three children boarded a train which deposited us at Poona. But Panchgani was still sixty miles away, far beyond the reach of any railway, and the only means of reaching it was to hire an open, battered Chevrolet. In this vehicle, driven at breakneck speed by a suicidal young Moslem, we plunged upwards, climbing the flanks of huge mountains, skirting precipices, the tyres slipping on the narrow track, until we reached our destination. We settled down in a small, primitive cottage with mud walls and concrete flooring, which overlooked the great downward slope of the mountain. Far below us lay the valley, bisected by the long sinuous line of the River Krishna, and beyond that the ramparts of yet other mountains. This was Mahratta country, an area of jagged peaks and lonely table-lands, created of black volcanic rock. The soil was red and fertile, covered with scrub and forest which abounded with panthers and jackals. The contrast between this wilderness and the bustle and heat of Bombay could hardly have been more striking. This was a land of narrow, twisting lanes, creaking bullock carts, and tiny, drowsy hamlets. Panchgani, with its single dusty street lined with tall trees, and half a dozen cramped, dark shops, seemed to belong to a special, peaceful world. The town consisted of a handful of Europeans and Anglo-Indians, a large convent which strove to educate about a hundred girls, and a somewhat smaller Protestant boys' school. The year that followed still remains in memory as an interlude of happiness and security. I explored every yard of the wild country around us, and even now, after a gap of nearly fifty years, I can still recall with affectionate accuracy each rocky plateau and narrow gorge.

By now I was nearly fifteen, tall and wiry, with a chin that even then displayed traces of an embryonic beard. I had started smoking and was constantly pilfering cigarettes whenever the opportunity arose; but as cigarettes were not always available, I constructed an enormous pipe, held together by masses of string and glue, which closely resembled the long, cumbersome peace pipes used by American Indians. I discovered a rocky cleft at the bottom of the garden which ensured complete privacy, and in this lair I sat contentedly exhaling great clouds of blue smoke from the bowl of this ridiculous instrument.

Because my mother was a devout Roman Catholic, our lives became increasingly involved with the convent, and in a matter of weeks I had fallen desperately in love with a girl of about my own age. She was a tall, graceful girl, with long legs, a mop of black hair, and green eyes, and for a long time she seemed the most important factor in my life. I suppose I can claim to be one of the few men to have been enrolled as a member of a senior girls' class in a Roman Catholic convent, but this, indeed, did occur. My mother could not accept the idea of sending us to the Protestant boys' school, and accordingly explained her difficulties to the Sister Superior, who after prolonged thought and prayer decided that this dilemma was sufficiently unusual to justify our admission to a purely feminine world. In the finish, my brother and I and two other Catholic boys swore a solemn oath never to exchange a single word with the girls who surrounded us, and on these terms were allotted desks at the extreme rear of the classroom.

I can truthfully report that we males sincerely tried to honour our share of the bargain, but unfortunately the girls refused to cooperate. As soon as the teacher was out of sight, we four interlopers were subjected to a barrage of ridicule that would have tried the patience of St Anthony. The girls would discuss our appearance and manners with a candour which soon proved to be more than we could bear. They indulged in an apparently serious evaluation of our defects: 'Which one of them is the ugliest?' or 'I notice the tall one hasn't washed this morning – as usual.' For three days we bore these indignities in stubborn silence. The first one to break was my brother. Provoked by some particularly scathing feminine wisecrack, he suddenly leapt to his feet, clutching a large book which he instantly flung at the head of his tormentor. Chaos ensued and within the course of the next hour our brief career as honorary girls came to an end.

I realized even then that my boyhood was slipping away, and that very soon I would be confronted by the more complicated pressures of an adult world. I did not look forward to this transition, but rather strove to prolong the dream-like, leisurely tempo of youth. I had few illusions about the world which awaited me. I had learnt almost as soon as I could speak that life was not to be trusted, that living, even at its best, was susceptible to indescribable horrors and injustice. But though I shrank from these uncertainties, I was also conscious of a fierce curiosity, a restless urge, to discover and confront the worst that existence could offer.

My sexual awareness was becoming increasingly powerful. Fantasies of love and pain dominated my imagination, and a single sentence in a book, or the momentary sight of a pair of graceful legs, would produce a violent erection which was the source of recurring embarrassment. This was the period when I read every book I could lay my hands on. I digested, more or less at a single gulp, the most unlikely subjects: a history of the Ottoman Turks, all of the novels written by Michael Arlen and Compton Mackenzie, and such titles as *A Ride to Khiva* which had remained unopened, gathering dust, on an upper library shelf, for more than fifty years. During the weekends I would wander for hours exploring distant plateaux or penetrating deep valleys overgrown with thick scrub.

I still remember one of these excursions very clearly, because it compelled me to examine the labyrinths concealed within myself. I did not start out until the late afternoon, and in less than an hour found myself in a narrow gorge, pushing my way past great black boulders that rose above the clumps of bamboo. A hyena suddenly emerged from a thicket within a yard of me, and loped away at a leisurely canter. I remember that the contrast between its weak, shrunken hindquarters, and its enormous savage head was oddly pathetic. A quarter of a mile further on, I passed a small, deserted Hindu temple, partially hidden by a grove of banyan trees. It looked forlorn and a little resentful, as though the ghosts of its neglected gods were still present, peering with watchful suspicion at an indifferent world. It was dark and strangely chill inside. A garland of withered marigolds and the fragments of a broken clay pot were the only signs of human occupation.

As I turned to leave, I noticed something scrawled in Urdu on the mottled wall. The writing was clear and bold, ornamented with numerous loops and curves. After several minutes I thought I had translated it fairly accurately. The message read, 'He who enters the Seventh Gate may not retrace his footsteps.' At first it seemed almost like nonsense, but the longer I thought about it, the more significant and disquieting did the words become. I felt inexplicably shaken, even a little afraid, as though this enigmatic warning was directed specifically towards myself and had been waiting patiently through the years for me to discover it in this forgotten shrine.

It was a relief to return to the light. Soon afterwards the ground sloped sharply downward, until it reached a point where the rockface ended abruptly in a cliff, forty or fifty feet above the jagged gorge. I scrambled forward, until I discovered a hollow close to the edge which formed a natural seat. I sat down, my legs folded under me, and lit one of my few remaining cigarettes. This eyrie overlooked a vast expanse of wild beauty. Under the high arc of the evening sky, jagged peaks and deep valleys stretched away as far as the eye could reach. The setting sun stained the rocks with a crimson glow, and it was as though the silent wilderness was eagerly awaiting the approach of night.

Completely isolated, and temporarily imprisoned by this enchanted solitude, my contact with reality suddenly dwindled until I was hardly conscious of my surroundings. What followed is difficult to describe, but in the course of the next few minutes my brain achieved a sensitivity, an intuitive awareness of the future which was not unlike a clairvoyant experience. I was looking towards the setting sun and the lonely wilderness, but I was hardly conscious of their existence. Instead, like a revelation, or a shaft of blinding light, a clear intimation of what awaited me in the years that lay ahead suddenly tore me apart. At that moment I knew the meaning of 'the Seventh Gate' and I glimpsed what, for me, would lie beyond it. I knew with absolute certainty that I was destined to explore the abyss, and penetrate regions of indescribable terror and happiness. I realized that my way would lead me close to hell and within touching distance of heaven, and that few would accompany me on this journey. I am still unable to explain those extraordinary minutes, but I remember distinctly that I never doubted the validity of my insight, and also – though this may seem inexplicable – accepted this future with fatalistic, shuddering resignation.

I wonder now what I would have done had this prophetic insight chosen to be more specific. If that boy, sitting alone in the twilight, had realized how most of his youth, and indeed of his life, was to be sacrificed to a sinister, merciless disease which would force him to live as a fugitive, and finally disfigure and blind him, I cannot now guess what his decision would have been. Perhaps a single step forward, and then the long drop to the rocky gorge below . . .

It may well seem rather improbable, but it is a fact that my first real sexual experience, my apple blossom memory of love, also occurred soon afterwards and must, however unlikely it may sound, be permanently associated with a large tin of sausages. I have always been aware that life has an incredible capacity for the incongruous, and the incident which I am going to relate is an almost perfect example of this truth. Luckier men may remember a moment of enchantment; two young bodies pulsating with passion, achieving paradise under starlit skies. My recollections of this supreme initiation only conjure up a kind of demented wrestling match in rain-soaked leaves, while I suffered acute agony from the pressure of that tin of sausages cutting into the small of my back.

I was not quite sixteen at the time and the woman involved was a school teacher named May Turner. We had met in the first place because my mother was convinced that my only chance of passing an exam known as the Senior Cambridge Certificate lay in receiving special coaching in mathematics. Miss Turner, a teacher at the local convent, was selected to undertake this task.

She was a tall, rather bony young woman of twenty-seven. I did not find her particularly attractive, but she had beautiful, lustrous brown eyes and graceful, soft hands. Her nose was a little large and, even worse, I considered that her legs were somewhat lacking in shape; still, she had an infectious laugh, a generous and kindly disposition, and I know now that she must have been an unusually likeable, innocent girl. She was animated and energetic, and every afternoon, at exactly 4.30, she would burst into our house with the violence of a small explosion. In theory, the two of us were now committed to mastering various abstruse mathematical problems for a period of an hour and a half. These lessons were carried out in a small room which opened onto our large veranda. Sitting side by side, on a low sofa, we faced a table impressively furnished with stacks of textbooks, pens and paper.

It is necessary to explain at this point that so long as we bent forward, scribbling energetically on the table, our heads and shoulders could be clearly seen by my mother as she sat sewing on the veranda outside; but if we leaned far back on the sofa we were momentarily concealed from my mother's watchful eyes by the angle of the doorway. This fact was to prove important, because very soon we had discovered an exercise considerably more entertaining that the pursuit of logarithms.

These unrehearsed efforts started soon after our first lesson. Miss Turner displayed a tendency to snuggle as close to me as possible, and when our heads drew close together, a strand of her thick, brown hair would tickle my face invitingly. Very soon afterwards her long-fingered, beautiful hands took to touching me in an extremely personal way. Within a matter of days we had given up even the pretence of work, and expended all our energies in a series of complicated acrobatics directed towards a pastime which had started long before mathematics.

These exchanges, because of the closeness of my mother, were extremely exhausting, both physically and emotionally. Like a couple of jerky puppets, we flung ourselves backwards and forwards between the table and the couch on which we sat. The ritual went something like this: first, the ostentatious pretence of work, during which our heads were clearly visible as we bent forward over the table. At this point it was scribble, scratch, the loud turning of pages. Then, a sudden spasmodic jerk backwards; kiss, suck, prod, tickle, followed by an equally feverish lunge that returned us to our original position. These furtive moments of bliss left me considerably the worse for wear. 'You look tired, dear,' commented my mother more than once, when

I staggered out onto the veranda in the wake of Miss Turner, my eyes glazed, hair dishevelled. I think now that Miss Turner enjoyed these interludes more than I did. I had to admit that she was nothing like the girl of my dreams, and although these erotic scuffles were certainly pleasurable while they lasted, they also left me with a sensation of acute frustration.

After a time, Miss Turner became very much a part of the family. She developed the habit of remaining after our lesson was finished and chatting with my mother till the late evening. In due course, her loud, husky voice, and the rapid clicking of her high heels, became a familiar part of our lives. Eventually she was invited to spend a long weekend at our bungalow, and early that same afternoon she appeared, grasping a small suitcase, and moved into our spare room. Everything pointed to a pleasurable visit, when suddenly a minor catastrophe descended upon us.

Our cook, and only servant, a tall, sullen Goan with dark, rolling eyes, named Joseph, decided to go on one of his periodic sprees. He returned to his kitchen soon after tea, swaying from side to side like a storm-tossed ship. He talked and gesticulated to some imaginary audience as he stumbled towards the kitchen door. Inside the kitchen we could hear him cursing and shouting, pausing occasionally to sing snatches of some ancient Goan song in a rich baritone. Soon afterwards he began to chase his wife round the kitchen, and the sound of her piteous shrieks was added to the confusion. The four of us, seated on the veranda, listened to this clamour with varying degrees of horrified fascination. Painful experience had taught us that in this mood Joseph represented a dangerous, unpredictable force, and all of us knew that any effort to restrain him could only produce fresh outbursts of incalculable violence. My brother, always a pessimist, said with sombre relish, 'My God, he's going to start playing on that damned fiddle,' and sure enough he had barely spoken when the eerie wails of a savagely inaccurate rendering of Dvorak's *Humoresque* proved that Joseph had indeed turned to his violin for solace. This final expression of defiance left us all deeply depressed, as it meant that this was no ordinary jag, and it would be useless to expect anything from our cook until the following morning.

'It doesn't look as though we're going to get anything to eat tonight,' said my mother and at this point my brother, no doubt anticipating what was to come, rose to his feet and disappeared. 'Does he often behave like this?' asked Miss Turner, to which, shaking her head sadly, mother replied, 'About once a month, generally, but he's not always as bad as this.' A melancholy silence followed, during which we all strove to adjust ourselves to a period of temporary starvation. Then my mother, never a character to accept defeat easily, brightened perceptibly. 'We've got plenty of eggs, and the small electric stove,' she remarked, and then she turned her head and looked at me speculatively. 'It's up to you, Peter,' she said. 'I'm afraid you'll just have to get to the bazaar and bring back a large tin of those nice sausages.'

I didn't like the sound of this idea. The bazaar was a good mile and a half away, and the prospect of a tramp across the country-side did not appeal to me at all. 'It's too late, the shops will all be closed,' I protested weakly, but my excuses were futile. 'Now, don't be lazy,' chided my mother severely. 'The walk will do you good, and you know very well that you're sure to find at least one shop open.' Realizing that further protests were useless, I rose to my feet and shuffled unwillingly towards the flight of steps that led to the garden. Just as I was on the point of disappearing, Miss Turner pulled herself out of her seat. 'Hold on a minute, and I'll go with you,' she said brightly, and very soon the two of us were walking together through the pale sunlight.

It had rained earlier in the day and drops of moisture still clung to the leaves and bushes, but the ground under foot was fairly dry. The distance to the bazaar could be greatly reduced by taking a short cut through a pine wood owned by no less a person than the Maharajah of Rajanpore, and this we proceeded to do. In availing ourselves of this detour, we were technically guilty of trespass, but as we had done so many times before without being challenged, we had no serious qualms.

Miss Turner's high heels were not particularly adapted to the rough track, and she wobbled along, clinging to my arm, apparently in high spirits. The bazaar looked forlorn, and almost deserted, but at last we discovered a shop that was not yet closed for the night, and I duly purchased a large oval tin of sausages. Clutching this tin, we left the shop and prepared to retrace our footsteps. By now the sun was almost below the horizon, and the surrounding hills were engulfed in the delicate light of the late evening. I was anxious to get home as soon as possible, but Miss Turner displayed a tendency to lag behind.

Now, it is essential to understand that at this stage nothing could have been further from my mind than the thought of making serious love to the woman beside me. Our crude efforts at snogging were strictly confined to the acrobatics performed on the sofa; she did not particularly appeal to me, and the possibility of venturing into more complicated aspects of love simply did not occur to me. After all, I had been brought up as a good Catholic boy, and the fact that she was not only considerably older than myself but also a teacher, exempted her in my mind from such ambitions.

When we reached the pine wood, the light had almost disappeared, and the track was in dark shadow. The long rows of pine trees looked sinister, and involuntarily we lowered our voices and advanced with as little noise as possible. Everything was very silent, except for the gentle murmur of the wind among the trees and the distant scuffle of some unknown creature in the undergrowth. Suddenly, Miss Turner gripped my arm, bringing me to a halt, as she leaned against me. In a whisper she explained that a pebble had got into her shoe, and she had to remove it.

The trunk of a fallen tree, partially concealed by a lush growth of ferns and bushes, lay half a dozen feet from the path a short distance ahead, just on the lip of a short, steep slope. With Miss Turner clutching my shoulder and limping awkwardly, we advanced towards this makeshift seat, and in another minute the two of us were seated side by side. As I sat staring sombrely into the gloom, Miss Turner bent forward, apparently engrossed in removing her shoe. This seemed to take quite some time, but at last she pulled herself erect, planted her foot firmly on the ground, and I assumed that we were now ready to continue our journey. Some moments of silence ensued, and then she suddenly stood up and began to dust her dress with the palm of her hand.

As I also prepared to get on my feet, she stepped forward quickly and flung her arms round my neck. This movement was not only completely unexpected but extremely uncomfortable. Her hands were clasped behind my neck, and as she pulled me forward, my nose and face were flattened against her stomach in such a fashion that breathing was almost impossible. Blinded and partially suffocated, I felt supremely foolish, but an innate courtesy compelled me to accept this unwanted caress with apparent enjoyment. Just as I was on the point of blacking out, a slight change in her position allowed me to turn my face a fraction of an inch, and so gulp a mouthful of much-needed air. Miss Turner spoke, but her voice sounded indistinct and far-away. I think she said 'You darling,' and although my mouth was still firmly embedded in the folds of her dress, I managed to croak dismally, 'You too.' After that the pace increased considerably, but this new fervour brought me scant relief. Like a pair of ill-matched dancers, we seemed incapable of executing a single movement that did not somehow go wrong. I was still seated and she was standing in front of and above me, so as she lowered her head and strove to kiss me passionately on the lips, most of her shots missed the target and landed on my eyes, my forehead and the side of my head. And when I, craning my neck at a painful angle, sought to return these caresses, her nose appeared to be constantly in the way, and all I could find was the tip of her ear, a bushy eyebrow, or the bottom of her chin.

This technique clearly left so much to be desired that we soon embarked on other, more exciting explorations. If I had only been satisfied to leave it like that, nothing except a slightly more ambitious form of snogging would probably have occurred. But always the little explorer, I was incapable of leaving well enough alone. I wish I could claim that what followed was due to uncontrollable desire, but in fact my sole motive was a kind of vague, clinical curiosity. There I was, close to the source, the ultimate mystery of life, and I could not resist further experimentation.

A little later Miss Turner began to tremble violently. And then suddenly she stepped back, paused for an instant and, like a stone from a catapult, flung herself into my arms. As our two bodies collided, my brain had just time to register the thought, 'My God, she's gone mad,' and then the force of the impact sent us both hurtling off the log and down the steep bank behind us. Our two bodies plunged downwards, in a wild mêlée of threshing arms and legs, until I hit bottom with a thud. Lying dazed on the hard, damp earth, I remember wondering vaguely whether I had broken my back.

I lay still with my eyes closed, until a series of grunts and heaves told me that Miss Turner was partially straddling my body, engaged in some sort of feverish activity. I opened my eyes unwillingly and caught a swift glimpse of her face looming directly above me. She looked completely mad, eyes wild, hair dishevelled, and a second later I realized that she was absorbed in the task of dragging me out of my trousers. With a sense of mingled horror and stupefaction, the thought crossed my mind, 'Heavens, I'm being raped,' and at that exact moment I became conscious of a grinding pain somewhere in the region of my shoulder blades. This unidentified pain increased each time the weight of her body, spreadeagled across my own, changed its position. Suddenly the explanation for this fresh problem became apparent. It was the tin of sausages. In some inexplicable fashion it had managed to lodge itself beneath my shoulders at an angle which forced the edge of the tin to gnaw ferociously into the small of my back.

I was suffering considerable agony, and yet I realized instinctively that this was hardly the moment to mention anything as mundane as a tin of sausages. But the pain increased, and finally I heard myself say, with incongruous prim formality, 'Excuse me, just a minute, if you don't mind.' At this request, Miss Turner paused abruptly and looked at me with astonished disbelief: 'What's that? What did you say?' I said reluctantly, 'It's that damn tin of sausages. It's wedged under my back. Do you mind if we get up a moment?'

Miss Turner exploded. She shouted at me in a high-pitched, hysterical voice, and her right hand shot out in an ineffectual effort to slap my face. A moment later her face crumpled and she began to cry, as she strove awkwardly to drag herself erect. But now I was conscious of a sudden flare of anger. I seemed to have got altogether more than my share of misfortune. First of all I had been sent flying through the air, then partially ravaged. After which I had suffered agony from the sausages, and now, as an ultimate humiliation, the woman was trying to slap my face. Miss Turner was on the point of scrambling away into the gloom when I leaned forward and gripped her ankle. If she wanted it, she was going to get it. And so at last, panting and wrestling in the wet foliage, I achieved my first experience of love.

I can't now remember much about my feelings at the time. It was not exactly enjoyable, and yet it was not particularly unpleasant either. All that it left in my mind is the smell of wet grass, sweat, scuffling, and rather extraordinary physical sensations. Taken all in all, I think the sausages gave me more real satisfaction when at last I ate them for supper.

12

After a year in Panchgani we returned to Bombay, and then moved on, first to Calcutta, and then to Delhi. I put Panchgani behind me with genuine regret, and my life in those lonely, beautiful mountains is a part of my boyhood that I can never forget. But, as always happened, immediately my father appeared, any semblance of peace and security was instantly dispelled. The advertising agency had passed away, more or less peacefully, several months earlier, and his restless, impatient spirit now led him to explore one city after another. He started a soap factory, bought a share in a sisal plantation, became the proprietor of a nightclub, and finished up as the manager of an organization dedicated to growing softwood timber in New Zealand. I am sure that he must have been involved with many other outlandish ventures, but these are all that I can recall for the moment.

Even then I realized that each new experiment led inexorably downwards. The man who had once been an important executive in a powerful organization was now reduced to squabbling with drunken soldiers outside a squalid cafe. He was still possessed by that private demon, that tragic obsession which had wrought such havoc in the past, and we were never allowed to forget it. Sinister rumours and barely concealed hostility followed him wherever he went. Slightly embarrassed policemen wearing enormous white topis and fearsome leather pistol-holsters called at the most unexpected moments to discuss his latest exploits. He was constantly summoned to appear before the small courts to answer the familiar charge, and a period of agonizing tension followed, during which he was involved in lengthy discussions with his Indian lawyers. In the end, he was either bound over, or fined, or succeeded in winning an acquittal, but however it went, anxiety and pain were unavoidable. It is impossible to estimate the consequences of these recurring horrors on my mother's sensitive, aloof personality, but I have no doubt that they were indirectly responsible for her early death a short time later. To the very end, she was able to confront the world with a tranquil stoicism which never failed to elicit sympathy and support, and nothing that happened could induce her to cut herself free from the lost cause she had unwittingly chosen to defend.

In 1927, the family, drifting slowly southwards, further and further away from the scenes of its earlier trials and defeats, finally reached a small town in the Nilgiris. The Nilgiris, or Blue Mountains as they were generally named by the local inhabitants, were a sparsely populated territory, almost completely isolated from the noisy crowded life of the plains. I can't remember now the exact reason for my father's decision to settle in this lonely outpost, but I suppose the choice was not really difficult to understand. He had by then worked his way through the greater part of the sub-continent and was now compelled to seek refuge in regions hardly known to the average citizen. We lived in a rambling bungalow surrounded by a large unkempt garden. Behind the house ran a small swift stream, which probably excused the incongruous name 'Burnside' with which the place was saddled. The bungalow was cold and decrepit, containing numerous dull, dark rooms sparsely furnished with rickety chairs and tables. But if 'Burnside' was old and sordid, its surroundings could hardly have been more beautiful. The town in which we lived stood many thousands of feet above sea level and consisted of little more than a straggle of seedy shops and a few dozen disgruntled houses perched wide apart on various rocky spurs. This was an area of deep green valleys and soaring mountain peaks. Wild arum lilies grew everywhere, their blossoms white and fleshy, and groves of eucalyptus trees covered the crest of each lonely hill. A huge lake, its waters smooth as silk, mirrored the surrounding ridges and was clearly visible from our garden. Nature here had a savage vitality, a greedy, implacable determination to survive, that was awe-inspiring. But the town itself lacked the charm and tranquillity of Panchgani. The Indians seemed discontented and apathetic, the white population morose and unfriendly.

My father had chosen to chance his luck as an auctioneer. He had built a large warehouse with a galvanized iron roof on what was called Commercial Road, and in this setting he held weekly auctions which produced little profit but much ill-will. He employed a hoary Indian clerk to assist him in the business, and this ancient passed his days pottering uncertainly round the twilit interior of the shed, flanked on all sides by every conceivable kind of junk. My father spent most of his time rushing about the countryside in a small, open two-seater. In this fashion he covered hundreds, possibly thousands of miles, calling upon the scattered local population in an effort to persuade them to part with anything suitable for his weekly auctions.

Unfortunately for him, the vast majority of these folk were not only very poor but intensely suspicious of flamboyant strangers, and consequently a long day's work would often produce only a rusty tin tub and a dozen tattered novels. These forays frequently resulted in violent quarrels, and in a matter of weeks father had succeeded in antagonizing a large number of his prospective clients. His language and behaviour when actually engaged in receiving bids were also severely criticized. He appeared to suffer from the delusion that he was an actor playing the lead in some soul-stirring drama, and would harangue his sullen audience with a flow of passionate invective guaranteed to excite resentment and hostility. After half a dozen such efforts, his role as an auctioneer gradually expired and eventually nothing was left except the forsaken shed and the doddering old clerk.

In the meantime, the rest of the family lived as best they could. For a time, my brother and I attended a local school which catered for the offspring of several denominations of Non-Conformist missionaries. Most of its pupils, which included both boys and girls, regarded us with undisguised suspicion and distaste, and I cannot remember exchanging a single friendly word with any of them. After one term I left the school and bid a final farewell to any sort of formal education.

When I recall this period of my life, I can only wonder at the extraordinary apathy displayed by my parents over the future of my brother and myself. There we were, strong but untried, two youths on the threshold of manhood, and the fact that we were completely unprepared for the world which awaited us never seemed to have occurred to either of them. One sundrenched month followed another; the rains came, then the cold weather, and as time hurried past we did little except lounge around the untidy garden, or stroll through the bazaar. During December and January it would become intensely cold, and we would use dried eucalyptus leaves to light log fires in the rusty iron grate which ornamented our living room. The sweet cloying odour of eucalyptus oil filled the room, and tiny, blue flames curled greedily round the burning logs. I played with Mary, now as vocal and self-willed as either of her brothers, for hours every day. Often the two of us would spend entire afternoons exploring the lonely uplands which surrounded us. We discovered an unoccupied, mysterious house which overlooked a dark lake, its waters thick as oil, reflecting the blurred shadows of the trees which encircled it.

Every Saturday, ancient movies were available at a place known as the Assembly Rooms, and Mary and I seldom missed them. The town possessed a surprisingly good library, and the two of us would visit it several times a week, returning laden with stacks of the most improbable and unsuitable kind of reading. A limp kitten, which rapidly became transformed into a sleek, pampered cat, attached itself to the family, and soon afterwards we adopted a mongrel dog named Scuffles. Books and old papers lay strewn all over the living room, and after a while my mother more or less gave up her efforts to get rid of them. Our only servant, a discontented young Tamil whose salary was always in arrears, carried out his duties with barely concealed hostility. Every now and then my father would appear with the most unlikely objects. Once it was a large picture in an ornate frame entitled *The Bath of Psyche*, which revealed a voluptuous, partially naked female pouring water over herself from a narrow ewer. Despite my mother's protests, he insisted on hanging this monstrosity above the mantelshelf, from which position it dominated the whole room.

When that first winter was over, our fortunes had never been lower. My father had more or less given up even the pretence of becoming an auctioneer. The shed remained but there was nothing inside it except the old clerk and an assortment of useless rubbish. Our income, always uncertain, dwindled to a pathetic standard. We fell into arrears with the rent and the servant's salary, and ran up ever-increasing bills at the local shop. My father sold his car, our silver tea service, and finally, one morning, when I entered the living room, I noticed with faint relief that *The Bath of Psyche* no longer hung above the mantelpiece. In all probability this picture served to feed us for at least a week.

My father's reaction to this situation was to keep out of the house for as long as he could. Sometimes he would disappear for several days, returning with explanations that ranged from the incredible to the fantastic. He would face my mother, apparently the embodiment of truth, his strong resonant voice producing long imaginary reasons for his absence. My mother, patient and resigned, listened to these legends with silent but obvious distrust. We all knew that he was almost certainly lying, but the possibility that just for once he might be telling the truth somehow increased our confusion. He became friendly with a large, noisy German family, notoriously shiftless and amoral, and took to spending long hours in their company. The rest of us adjusted ourselves to this abnormal life as best we could, while my mother doggedly continued to maintain something that resembled a home. My brother and I seldom spoke to each other. We slept in the same room, ate at the same table, but as we grew older our personalities grew apart. We all knew that this kind of life could not last much longer, but in the meantime all we could do was surrender ourselves to this unreal, pointless world.

And then, my mother, the one reliable point in our treacherous, changing world, seemed suddenly to falter, as though the long, frustrating years had finally exhausted her. She became pale and listless and complained of severe, recurring pains in the stomach. After a couple of months she was taken to the local hospital and examined by a woman doctor. This idiot, with unbelievable stupidity, diagnosed acute indigestion and advised her to take a daily walk of at least two miles. Accordingly, my unfortunate mother, credulous and docile to the last, forced her weary, sick body to cover the prescribed distance when each step must have been torture. After another few weeks had elapsed, and her condition had clearly worsened, another doctor of a very different calibre was called in. Dr Long was efficient and energetic, radiating vitality and optimism. He visited the house one hot afternoon, and was shown into my mother's room. When he emerged, his plump, good-humoured face had become grave. He took my father aside, and told him bluntly that my mother was suffering from an advanced state of cancer. He suggested an immediate operation, but the expression in his eyes and the tone of his voice indicated all too clearly that he had little hope for the future.

The months which followed were darkened by continuous anxiety. Outside the house the hills were bathed in radiant sunshine, but inside there was nothing but a twilit world dominated by sickness and fear. My mother was sent to Madras, where she underwent a particularly cruel and degrading operation. Three months later she returned, wasted and pallid, hardly more than a ghost of what she once had been.

And now, all that was left was to await the inevitable, cruel finale. Dr Long appeared every day to administer the injections of morphia which temporarily defeated the onslaught of unbearable pain. He would burst onto our veranda like a gust of wind, evoking smiles and high spirits. He would chatter away to my mother, exuberant and irresistible, until at last we would hear her laugh. By now we were receiving weekly cheques from her opulent half-sister, without which we could hardly have survived. Mrs Beck, as she now called herself, was the only member of my mother's family to achieve a considerable degree of social standing and financial stability. She was then in her early forties, and after a youth dedicated to the capture of two husbands and the enjoyment of several lovers, had finally decided to settle down to a life of delayed respectability. Her current husband, Norman Beck, was a personage of considerable importance, a member of the ICS, who was said to possess a brain of dynamic force and energy. It was even whispered that Mr Beck might possibly become the Governor of a Province, supposing his career continued its upward trend. I had only met my exotic aunt once but I knew that my mother and she had kept up a desultory correspondence across the years.

And so those dreadful last months slipped slowly past. My

mother sat in the bright sunshine, smiling and uncomplaining, still capable of gentle irony and even laughter. She had no illusions about the future, but I think that by then she was not averse to the prospect of death.

One chill night, my father shook me awake from a deep sleep. It must have been about 2 a.m. and a strong wind was beating against the windows. As I opened my eyes, still partially stupefied by sleep, he said roughly, 'If you want to say goodbye to your mother, you'd better come now.' His voice sounded angry and bitter, as though he was threatening an enemy. I pulled myself out of bed and dragged myself into a dressing-gown. The house was silent, but I could imagine only too well the scene that awaited me, in that other room. My heart and brain were numbed with pain and horror. I shrank from surrendering myself to the ordeal, the dark misery of death, which threatened to engulf me. Each separate nerve and muscle shrank from the terror of peering into the face of death, struggled to avoid the stench of sickness and dissolution.

Now, I have never been particularly susceptible to convictions of personal guilt or sin. I believe that when all the circumstances of my life are taken into consideration, I have done little for which I need feel real shame. I have frequently erred in judgement and action, but as a general rule such failings have harmed nobody but myself. But on that windy night, as I stood uncertainly by my bed, waiting to see my mother for the last time, I believe I did succumb to a sin of real magnitude. I remember that in those few moments, realizing exactly what I was doing, I selfishly chose to evade a challenge to my heart and imagination, which should never have been rejected. Because I lacked the courage to bear my part of the pain and horror which confronted me, I chose to deny its existence. Like a fish slipping into a pond, I allowed my mind to dissociate itself. I retreated, as it were, into the safety and indifference of my strong youthful world, detaching myself from the pity and sorrow which seemed more than I could bear. I stood beside my mother's bed, looking down at her shrunken, pain-racked body. Her face was wet with sweat, and though her eyes were partially open, I knew that she was no longer conscious of the life around her. Every few seconds a spasm of agony pierced her waxen yellow flesh. I bent forward and kissed her forehead. The skin I touched was moist, and yet deeper down I could feel the fever which consumed her.

I went through all the motions of a sorrowing, heart-broken son, but below the surface I was in hiding, skulking behind the barrier of cowardly rejection. My mother died a few hours later, and when I next saw her, all that was left was a caricature of what had once been living flesh. Her body lay neatly arranged on her bed, the face as still as stone, her hands folded across her breast. Masses of arum lilies had been spread over the bed, and their sweet, oddly corrupt odour permeated the room. Strangers passed in and out of the house. Nothing much was said, and my father, pale but stoical, seemed little more than another interloper. She was buried late the following evening, her body carried to the cemetery on a clumsy hand-cart pushed by half a dozen men. It had become very dark, the air cold and damp, when we reached the church. An unseen bell tolled monotonously, and the shadowy figure of a priest emerged to read the burial service. It was all over astonishingly soon, and the four of us returned to the empty house. There seemed nothing to say.

A week later, a prim, watchful Indian woman appeared. She had been sent halfway across India from the convent in Panchgani to collect Mary and hand her over to the care of the nuns. In a matter of hours her few possessions were packed, and the little girl was ready to depart. Holding the Indian woman's arm with one hand, and clutching a novel by Rider Haggard in the other, her diminutive figure vanished from my sight. Eight eventful years had to pass before I saw her again.

After Mary's departure, what was left of the family accepted an increasing and chaotic disorder. The three of us, marooned in that large, untidy bungalow, lived together like strangers compelled by some unforeseen calamity to share the same roof. My father seldom appeared, and my brother and I hardly exchanged a word. All of us were aware that we had come to the end of a chapter, but none of us could guess what destiny proposed to do with the future. The weeks that followed had a restless, dreamlike quality. Our servant had disappeared and his place was taken by a sullen old Tamil who viewed us with undisguised suspicion. On those infrequent occasions when the three of us were together, the tension produced was almost insupportable. My father's grief had been replaced by a savage impatience which was frequently released in outbursts of illogical fury. My brother seemed to bring out all that was worst in his character, and when they spoke they were almost instantly entangled in futile arguments.

One evening the two of them started an absurd, interminable controversy during which my father bellowed at my brother and my brother, cold but inflexible, refused to capitulate. I can see them now, facing each other across the chilly, disordered room: my father, crimson with rage, gesticulating wildly towards my brother's pale, youthful face. It went on and on, its original cause completely forgotten, as it produced a dozen fresh issues, all of them equally crazy and unnecessary. In the finish, somewhere about midnight, goaded beyond endurance, father suddenly rose to his feet, sprang towards my brother, and slapped him hard across the face. By this time I was also on my feet, and involuntarily, as his hand crashed against my brother's face, I heard myself yell out in protest. He turned with unexpected speed. For a split second I saw his eyes, dilated with rage, glaring at me, and then he stepped forward and struck me a quick glancing blow on the side of the jaw. It did not hurt me, and the thought of reprisal never entered my mind, but I realized, with a shock of horrified disbelief, that he had thought I was on the point of attacking him, and had actually been afraid of what I might do. I just stood there and looked at him, and after a while his eyes slid away from my glance. Without a word he left us. Silence returned, and with it the time for regret and appraisal. We all knew that what had just occurred represented something very close to the ultimate in degradation. My father never apologized for this incident, for it was not in his nature to admit that he was wrong, but we both knew that he was, in fact, deeply ashamed of his part in it.

Weeks later, I returned to the house late one evening. There was no sign of my brother or my father, and as I entered the living room, I saw the little old clerk from the auction rooms hovering in the shadows. He handed me an envelope, and inside was a brief note in my father's familiar handwriting. It said, 'I've got to get out of this bloody country. Here is 50 rupees. Best of luck.' And that was all.

13

By the time I reached my twentieth birthday, I had already succeeded in losing not less than seven different jobs. In rapid succession I had tried my hand at selling cars and operating a record
showroom; I had attempted to run the sports department in a
large retail shop, sold advertising space for a railway timetable,
and worked for a short period as a somewhat unconvincing clerk
in one of the leading firms in South India. There must have been
several other ventures which I can no longer remember. The
essential fact to record is that I was a complete and utter failure.

This was hardly surprising, because I realized even then that
business in all its varied aspects bored me to extinction. I was unable to develop the least enthusiasm for the tasks which society
apparently considered it essential for me to perform. I could not
have cared less whether some ambitious shopkeeper decided to
buy three hundred records, or whether a wealthy Indian purchased half a dozen expensive tennis rackets. I felt instinctively
that achievements of this kind could never fill the aspirations of
my heart.

I lived like a nomad, moving from one city to another, existing
in seedy hotels or in shoddy rooms where I seldom remained for
more than a few weeks at a time. But the odd fact is that I was
happy, and that I never thought of myself as either a failure or a
misfit. My unquenchable optimism assured me that there were
better days ahead, and that sooner or later I would escape from
the frustrating, sterile environment which then surrounded
me.

In the meantime, I was content to read, dream, make firm
friendships, and implacable enemies, while I explored the vast,
unpredictable labyrinths of India. At this stage of my life, the
complications, heartbreaks and rewards of love were still an unexplored territory. I was constantly obsessed by the demands of
sex, but the thought of any permanent relationship with a girl
never even occurred to me. I was satisfied to respond to the fugitive, short-lived adventures of the road, and these were not par-

ticularly difficult to find, either by luck or the simple expedient of disgorging a few rupees.

When father deserted us, our future prospects could hardly have been less encouraging. There we were, hardly more than boys, marooned in an empty bungalow, surrounded by unpaid bills and all the other consequences of my father's ineptitude. Nobody knew what to do with us. Neither of us had received even the most elementary training that could have helped us to earn a living, and our entire psychological background had conditioned us to regard such mundane problems with contempt and distaste. Despite our lack of funds, education, and almost everything else, we had been brought up to believe that the Greaves possessed certain special gifts which, in due course, must be recognized by the world.

Our only wealthy relative, my mother's half-sister who was married to a Collector in Dacca, was called in to discuss the emergency. We lunched with her at a hotel in Coonoor, in an atmosphere of cold embarrassment. With an obvious lack of enthusiasm, she offered to pay our fare to Australia. 'You should really do very well out there,' she said vaguely, 'there are those enormous sheep farms, and cattle stations, and so on.' Neither my brother nor I was impressed by this proposal. We both realized that her real objective was to get rid of us, and somehow, despite my vivid imagination, I was unable to picture myself making an outstanding success as a kind of father figure to hordes of unresponsive sheep. My brother had the sense to say very little, but I, always addicted to a dangerous fluency, talked and laughed with misplaced confidence. As the meal progressed I could feel her initial distaste developing into hostility. She just didn't like me, and I had neither the experience nor the desire to change her feelings. At the finish, she opened her expensive bag and reluctantly handed me the equivalent of about ten pounds.

It was clearly impossible to earn a living in a tiny hill station, so our first move was to reach Madras, the only large city in that part of the country. For about a week we occupied a huge, dark room in the residence of the Roman Catholic Bishop of Mylapore. I cannot now remember exactly how this was achieved, but I presume our local priest must have written to His Grace on our behalf. I don't think we ever saw the bishop, but dealt instead with his secretary, a pale, good-looking young Jesuit whose lips perpetually gripped a large, evil-smelling cigar. This young man was a Portuguese, and from the onset communication between us was far from easy. He would listen to us in silence, his eyes downcast, face expressionless, as the smoke from his cigar drifted slowly towards the ceiling. From his point of view we must have seemed alien creatures, not easily subservient to the authority of the Church, capable of expressing opinions that were both dangerous and immoral; he also disliked the British very deeply, and these feelings did nothing to ease our relationship.

In some way His Grace managed to put up with us for a week. Naturally we were expected to attend Mass every morning, and as we were always late, a great part of the secretary's time was devoted to prodding us in the direction of the chapel. One afternoon, he happened to drop into our room while I was reading an American magazine decorated with a picture of a tall beautiful girl in a bathing costume. He took the magazine from my hands, and for a long minute stood gazing thoughtfully at the picture. Finally with barely suppressed distaste, he put the paper down, expelled a thick cloud of smoke, and said very quietly, 'I do not think you will be happy here. Perhaps it would be better to find other accommodation.' And with those two brief sentences, the Vatican, with all its pomp and wisdom, unofficially dissociated itself from the lives of the two young Greaves.

For the next four months we lived in a damp, cramped go-down on the outskirts of the city. Now, we had almost reached the economic level of the indigenous population. We had no bathroom, and could only bathe in the nearby river. We applied for work, any kind of work, all over the city, but without success. Because we were white, and spoke without an instantly recognizable chee chee accent, the large organizations like the railways and customs, who offered employment to thousands of young Anglo-Indians, refused to consider us. And the fact that we had not been brought up in England, and were also completely unqualified, eliminated the higher paid posts. Furthermore, the slump of the thirties was beginning and jobs were becoming harder and harder to find. I realize now that the odds against us were so steep that the only real wonder is that we survived at all.

At last, when we had almost crossed the line that divides poverty from utter destitution, we managed to get ourselves taken on by a thriving car agency in Mount Road. Our official designation was apprentice salesmen, and we were first supposed to spend a couple of years mastering the secrets of the internal combustion engine, after which we could become trained and efficient members of the selling staff. The snag was that our salary during this training period amounted to a mere pittance; just remaining alive was still a problem.

We had been lucky enough to find comparatively comfortable accommodation in a YMCA hostel. This was a large, old-fashioned house, whose grounds included tennis courts and other sporting facilities, but its outstanding merit from my point of view was its astonishing reluctance to eject residents who failed to pay their bills. In this respect, the secretary displayed a truly biblical generosity and understanding, and the fact that I still owe this kindly establishment a considerable sum of money compels me to record, even at this late date, my gratitude for all it did for me. The hostel accommodated about a dozen men, mostly youngsters like myself, but also several ancients in their late thirties who had lived there for many years. My brother and I were installed in a huge, oblong room, which we shared with two others. The room was furnished with stark simplicity, a bed at each corner and a large table in its centre. There were no fans, and the nights were unbearably hot and airless, but nevertheless I still remember with real pleasure the eighteen months I spent there.

My career as a trainee car salesman was brief and inglorious. I seemed to be perpetually smeared with oil and grease, and a great part of my time was spent lying under a variety of cars, staring fixedly at a complicated assortment of nuts and bolts a couple of inches above my nose. The firm boasted a luxurious showroom, in which the sleek, expensive cars waited in aloof dignity, surrounded by potted palms and large polished desks; but we were seldom allowed to enter this opulent section. I learnt just two singularly uninspiring skills during the months that followed. The first was the ability to drive a car backwards with extraordinary skill and efficiency; I cannot claim any special flair for driving in the usual direction, but stern-wise my skill was undisputed. I also mastered the art of jacking up a car with considerable dexterity, but I must admit with shame that otherwise my knowledge of cars remained strictly limited.

For the first time in my life, I was compelled to work closely with Indians, and I was pleasantly surprised to realize that they were astonishingly like other human beings. One of their senior drivers was a tall, temperamental Moslem named Edrice. He wore a red fez, and attacked everything he did with a furious energy, gesticulating and cursing at the cars as though they were living creatures determined to oppose him. Another driver was a Tamil with a name that sounded something like Annoppill-swami. He was plump, placid and good-natured, and worked happily and methodically, laughing and chatting to anybody who happened to be near. The Sales Manager was a tall, suave Englishman who was always immaculately dressed and wore a flower in his buttonhole. I was the target of his wrath on several occasions, but I think now that he must have been an unusually kindly soul to have tolerated my numerous shortcomings for as long as he did.

After the first couple of weeks I was heartily sick of everything that even remotely resembled a car, and my zest for work rapidly decreased. Whenever possible I remained at home, claiming in rapid succession to be bed-ridden by malaria, ear-ache, piles, a severe cold, and a variety of other sinister aches and pains. Once away from work, I relapsed immediately into a state of blissful content. Alone in that large, sunlit room, I would sprawl across my bed, reading and smoking for hours at a stretch. I belonged to a small lending library, which unfortunately stood very close to the car showroom, and on one occasion when I was supposed to be lying prostrate, burning with fever, I ran into the Sales Manager as I left the library, my arms loaded with a stack of books. I dived back through the doorway, and I could tell by the puzzled expression on his face that he was trying to decide whether he was suffering from some kind of hallucination.

At the end of six months, to everybody's relief, it was decided that I lacked the special aptitude essential to selling cars.

My second job was altogether more promising. A firm selling gramophone records had built a brand-new showroom on Mount

Road. By a stroke of almost miraculous good luck, one of their directors decided that I was exactly the kind of young man to make a success in the record business. After several interviews, I was offered what then seemed to me the colossal salary of three hundred rupees a month, and was told that I would be expected to take charge of the showrooms. For the first time in my life I felt really important, and marched towards my new assignment bursting with enthusiasm and confidence.

For a while I was happy enough. The showroom was sleek and decorative, and my 'work' hardly justified the name. I loved music of every description, and to be paid for listening to it seemed almost too good to be true. Every now and then a customer would drift across the threshold, and I would be expected to discuss the latest releases and demonstrate the various gramophones available. This was a chore I greatly enjoyed; the oddest people came through our doors, and as I was naturally talkative and curious, these exchanges were often a real pleasure.

My downfall, when it came, was swift and irrevocable. Like a chain-reaction, half a dozen small mistakes joined together to produce a single explosion. When I left the showroom on the evening it all happened I had no premonition of disaster; in fact my work had gone unusually well. I had succeeded in selling not only thirty or forty small records but also two large albums, one of Gilbert and Sullivan, the other of Beethoven's Piano Concertos. A director from Head Office had even taken the trouble to phone through and personally express his approval of my efforts. I felt unusually happy as I waited for the rest of the staff to take themselves off before I carefully locked the heavy metal doors which led into the showroom.

The evening was cool and peaceful. On the other side of the street, more or less directly opposite the showroom, stood a shabby bar named the Pagoda Tavern, and on an impulse I decided to go in and celebrate the triumph of the day. Inside, I met a young soldier from the Middlesex Regiment which was then stationed in Madras. He was drinking Japanese beer, and as he seemed eager to chat, there was little I could do except sit down at his table and order a bottle for myself. We exchanged half a dozen desultory comments, and then he started to speak about his life before he joined the Army. He was soon extolling the joys of London, including the delights of real English beer compared to the diluted bat's pee they served in this godforsaken slum. I have no idea why I should have wanted to defend the output of a Japanese brewery, but before I knew what I was doing we had become involved in an absurd drinking contest, matching each other glass for glass. This might have resulted in nothing worse than a sore head, but after we had put down the first five bottles a third party joined our table, and it was he who was to lead me towards the final catastrophe.

This man was an Armenian pimp named Jeremiah, and I was to discover later that almost everybody in the city, apart from my innocent self, was well aware of his devious ways and left him severely alone. He sat down, gazing at me benignly, his lips curved into a discreet smile. After a time he leaned forward and began to whisper persuasively into my left ear. 'Why must you waste all your money on beer? What you need is a woman, and I know a girl, she's only sixteen, never touched by a man, you could have her for only five rupees.' I was instantly interested. My brain was not at its best, but it did occur to me that a young and beautiful virgin might indeed be better than a bottle of tepid Japanese beer.

By now the lights and the furniture were swaying slightly, but I managed to get to my feet. Jeremiah led the way through the dark silence. The fresh air temporarily cleared my mind, but after a minute of comparative sobriety, drunkenness returned with increased power. I discovered that I could still articulate more or less clearly, but that my legs were no longer to be relied upon. I rolled from side to side like a ship adrift in a heavy sea, and once I would have fallen heavily had not Jeremiah stretched out his arm.

The five hours that followed were a combination of dazzling light and inky darkness. Fireworks seemed to explode inside my head. Instead of being led to the beautiful, sixteen-year-old virgin, I found myself inside a grimy brothel. Here I soon succeeded in getting myself involved in a fight with several other men, and was finally ejected into the bosom of the kindly night. As I shot through the air, the knowledge that I had been able to present one of my enemies with a magnificent black eye was extremely gratifying, but I was to pay dearly for this temporary elation when I learnt that I had succeeded in clouting no less a person than the Managing Director of one of the city's most influential firms. I picked myself up from the pavement, hailed a rickshaw, and headed towards a large hotel. Here I met a young planter, whose temperament and convictions were exactly adapted to my own. Together we drank half a dozen martinis, two crème de menthes and several large whiskies.

I was now about as drunk as any human being could be, and from this point onwards time, space, and action became inextricably confused. The young planter suddenly disappeared, and I found myself staggering about outside a large dance hall, blazing with light, and vibrating with the sound of music. Plunging across the threshold, I began to walk rather uncertainly across the crowded dance floor. The beauty of the women, and the immaculate evening dress of the men made an overpowering appeal to my aesthetic sense. I smiled fatuously as I advanced, warmed by a powerful but misguided conviction that my fellow humans were not only supremely attractive but endowed with hearts of pure gold. In this mood it seemed reasonable enough to stretch out my arm and bestow numerous fatherly pats on the naked backs of the women prancing about in my direct vicinity. It was disappointing to realize that these spontaneous caresses failed to evoke a corresponding warmth in the females. Instead, muffled shrieks, protesting scowls, and swift movements clearly directed towards avoiding my presence were too marked to be disregarded. Tears sprang to my eyes, and the acceptance of human injustice was both bitter and painful. Such reflections were short-lived, however, because almost immediately, with savage efficiency, strong hands grasped my shrinking frame, and once again I was flung into an unsympathetic world.

But my appetite for pleasure refused to be suppressed. In some fashion which is no longer clear to me, I became attached to a group of noisy young merchant sailors, almost as drunk as myself. Encouraged by these reinforcements, I attempted to enter the dance hall for the second time, and when my path was blocked, instantly aimed a tremendous punch – which missed its target by about two feet – at the head of the man obstructing me.

The sailors joined in the fray, and all I can remember of the next few minutes is the thudding of fists and the scramble of colliding bodies. Suddenly the lights went out, and a few seconds later I found myself surrounded by half a dozen Tamil policemen who seized various parts of my body with quite unnecessary force, lifting me high above the floor. In this position, temporarily airborne, so to speak, I continued to kick and squirm with undiminished energy. Inevitably I was overpowered, and within the space of a very few minutes a single quick shove sent me flying inside a small, barred cell at the local Police Station.

The next morning, feeling completely refreshed, I was escorted to the courts to appear before a gnarled old Indian magistrate, who sentenced me to a fine of ten rupees or one week's protective custody. I searched my pockets carefully, but found nothing except a single rupee note. I don't know what would have happened then, had not a kindly European police sergeant come forward to pay my fine, and then drive me home in the side-car of his motorcycle.

After he had been paid, I hurried to get myself washed and into clean clothes. It was only then that the full horror of my situation became clear. I looked at my watch: its hands pointed to half past ten. I remembered that I held the only available keys to the showroom, and the entire staff must have been waiting outside for the last hour and a half. I could not imagine – I did my best *not* to imagine – what they were likely to do in these circumstances.

I had recently bought myself a small two-stroke motor-cycle, and on this ridiculous vehicle I rode towards the showrooms. Mount Road was broad, straight and empty, and I could see them when I was still several hundred yards away. There they were, the entire staff, waiting patiently in the bright morning sunlight. Somebody had got chairs for the two senior men and they sat there, silent and forlorn, framed by the standing figures of the two Tamil clerks, each of whom was holding an umbrella, and the plump bearer in his khaki uniform. Not a word was said as I puff-puffed slowly into view. The silence remained unbroken as I dismounted and walked stiffly to the closed front door. I could feel their eyes on my back as I bent down to insert the key, and as the door flung open they all trooped past me with the sombre dignity of mourners at a wake. An hour later I was summoned to Head Office and instantly and violently fired.

About three years and seven jobs later, my father suddenly reappeared. He looked older and slightly pathetic, his hair streaked with grey, his face creased with fatigue and depression. So much had happened since we were last together that he seemed like a stranger, and when we faced each other I could think of nothing to say. There was no place for him in our young, hopeful world, and with a cruelty that might well have been a kind of unconscious revenge, neither my brother nor I did anything to help him. He actually got himself booked into our hostel, and I can still remember the sight of his lonely, gaunt figure sitting at our table, observing but not participating in the jokes and chatter of my youthful companions. His clothes were worn and ill-fitting and he was clearly hard up and considerably chastened. I gathered that he had spent a year in Australia, then several months in Rangoon, but I never did learn exactly what he had been up to. He only stayed a couple of days, after which he packed his shabby suitcase and slipped away with hardly a word.

But if I believed that at long last his energy and effrontery had deserted him, I was soon to learn that he was not to be so easily written off. Some months later he wrote to me from Calcutta. He had started a new business and – what was even more astonishing – was apparently earning considerable sums of money. It also seemed that he had suddenly become conscious of his obligations to his family, because he went on to say that if I decided to return to Calcutta he would guarantee to support me for at least six months. I learnt that Mary, now a girl of seventeen, had left the convent and was living with him in his small flat overlooking Dalhousie Square. I managed to scrape together my fare to Calcutta, and very soon afterwards found myself facing him across a desk in his untidy, noisy office.

I was startled and not particularly pleased when I heard that he proposed to offer me a job in his mysterious business. I had not the least desire to become involved with any of his short-lived, reckless adventures, but the fact was that I lacked the courage to tell him so. 'I'm offering you a real chance to make good,' he assured me smugly. 'You can start at the bottom and work your way right up to the top, and you can always depend on me to help you with all I've learned about business during the last thirty years.' 'Thank you, thank you very much,' I heard myself say wearily, and the very next morning my career as a Junior Executive in H. Greave Ltd got under way.

My father and his partner, a retired Lieutenant-Colonel, were involved in a series of enterprises, each one of which was more improbable than its predecessor. For example, within a few days of my enlistment, the two of them succeeded in selling a railway siding plus several components of rolling stock which simply did not exist. Not only did they succeed in finding a buyer, they also accepted a large deposit for the delivery of these phantom commodities.

My father had an Indian broker named Raju Lal who constantly fed him with the most improbable fragments of information. One morning this man hurried into the office, bursting with enthusiasm. He had discovered a derelict siding owned by the East India Railway, about two hundred miles from the city, hidden in a patch of thick jungle. His information was completely reliable: he had personally interrogated the man who had stumbled across this forgotten site, and according to him the railway would be only too glad to sell the equipment for a mere song. My father listened to this fable with the credulity of a child. Within a matter of minutes he had rung up a large American oil company, and offered them two small locomotives, both in perfect working order, six standard goods wagons and a hundred feet of concrete platform. The oil company displayed immediate interest and within a matter of days had paid out a deposit of five thousand rupees, pending inspection. Of course, when my father and Raju Lal attempted to locate the stock, they were unable to discover anything that even distantly resembled a concrete platform, locomotives, or anything else.

A month later, I was almost drowned in the Bay of Bengal as a direct consequence of yet another of these ventures. In this case, father bought a deep-sea dredger named the *Chandpore* from the port authorities in Chittagong. He succeeded in getting the vessel for a nominal sum and instantly sold it to a Japanese firm who intended to break it up and sell it as scrap. Once again he accepted a large deposit, something like 50,000 rupees, and blithely agreed to deliver the craft to the Calcutta docks. When I tried to point out that it might be a little difficult to bring this ancient vessel across two hundred miles of open sea, H G brushed aside my doubts with explosive contempt: 'Don't talk like a bloody fool. Chittagong isn't at the other end of the world; it's only across the bay. God damn it, a half-witted three-year-old could steer her across that little bit of sea.'

My misgivings turned out to be only too well-founded. H G's idea was that the vessel should be towed across the bay, but not a single shipping company was prepared to accept this responsibility. My father raged and fumed, quarrelling furiously with various marine superintendents, and was soon convinced that the entire nautical world was joined together in a sinister conspiracy to defeat him. Finally, driven to desperation, he decided to recruit his own crew and bring her down without outside help. In one of the local brothels he stumbled across an alcoholic Scot who possessed a First Engineer's Certificate. This man was nearly seventy and had not been inside an engine-room for at least twenty years, but when he was temporarily sober the offer of several hundred rupees and half a dozen bottles of whisky induced him to agree to travel to Chittagong. The skipper was a half-caste Frenchman who called himself Captain Chopin. This man was nervy and talkative, and looked more like an out-of-work bookie than a stalwart old sea-dog, but the fact that he also had not been in command for many, many years did not prevent my father from employing him. I was sent to Chittagong, representing the owners, to supervise the voyage to Calcutta.

After several weeks of unbelievable toil and sweat, the *Chandpore* actually put to sea. She steamed confidently out of Chittagong, but less than twenty-four hours later she was rolling helplessly in a heavy swell, her engines dead. The wind was rising alarmingly and it was obvious even to me that really dangerous weather was blowing up. The terrified Lascars howled, 'Allah! Allah!' and the valorous Captain Chopin placed himself in a kneeling posture, intoning several colourful Catholic prayers addressed to the Virgin Mary. I was scared out of my wits, and must admit that I did little to attempt to change our skipper's mind when he decided that further progress was impossible and that it was absolutely necessary to return to Chittagong.

This was the last time my father succeeded in involving me in any of his commercial fantasies. Soon afterwards we parted by mutual consent, and I still remember the sensation of relief as I hurried out of that lunatic office for the last time.

14

In one of the narrow side streets of Calcutta, set in a high wall, was a clumsy wooden gate that led into a paved courtyard on one side of which stood a squat, decrepit old bungalow. It was in this improbable setting that some of the most ecstatic and important events of my life took place.

A broad dusty veranda faced the courtyard, neglected and empty except for an old black spaniel, perpetually chained, and a vicious cockatoo imprisoned in a large rusty cage suspended from the wall. The ancient courtyard, scorching under the sunlight, and the deserted veranda beyond, always appeared to be somnolent, almost lifeless. I soon learnt that this aura of inertia was in fact completely deceptive. The old house had been the setting for unbelievable scenes of passion and lunacy, and even now these feverish currents still persisted.

Its presiding genius was a thin, bent old woman named Miss Carter, whose small petulant face expressed an unchanging disapproval of everything around her. She was perpetually on the move, scurrying from one room to another like an old witch, her bloodless lips clenched round a cigarette, which invariably pointed upwards at an aggressive angle. Miss Carter was the centre of a whirlpool of frenzied turbulence, because of her flair for surrounding herself with the most extraordinary people and offering them a refuge in her domain. Villains of every description, drug addicts, ex-convicts, alcoholics, public school types who had been drummed out of the British army, all, propelled by some instinctive force, clustered under Miss Carter's roof to rest and recuperate. She never asked them to pay, and some of them never did, and yet, surprisingly enough, a considerable proportion of them returned when their fortunes had improved to make good everything they owed. Miss Carter was, in fact, a practising

Christian, who did not accept Christianity and constantly proclaimed her atheistical convictions.

The lives of these lodgers were completely unpredictable. Some stayed a matter of days, others for years, but as a general rule the inhabitants of this battered caravanserai were constantly either coming or going. When I joined their ranks, they consisted of a portly, distinguished middle-aged man named Sheridan-Cowley, who claimed to have been to Eton, and was said to possess the largest sexual organ in Bengal. After him, came an old, old woman, so bent and shrunken that she seemed to be partially mummified. This old girl was a genuine mainliner, who had been addicted to morphia ever since her early youth. It was said that she had once been unbelievably beautiful, but this seemed almost impossible to accept when one looked at her now. There was also an ancient Bengali woman, tall and brittle, named Mary Chittor. She was an uncompromising nymphomaniac, relatively rich, who had wasted the greater portion of her wealth on a series of unscrupulous lovers, all of whom fleeced her without mercy.

But not all the inhabitants of Number 7 Salem Lane were old and degenerate. There was also the sound of youthful laughter, an exuberant voice shattering the silence, rapid footsteps moving from one room to the next, all emanating from a young woman who was said to be Miss Carter's niece. Her name was Sharon, and despite her splendid red hair, her jade green eyes, and the pallor of her smooth white skin, somewhere deep inside her was the dark colour of India. I knew this because I had seen her grandmother, an ancient shapeless crone with a fatuous smile, and a skin so dark that there could be no doubt. Sharon's mother too, though almost fair enough to pass as an Italian, was also unmistakably 'tainted' –and it was then considered a taint – by the presence of a darker race.

Sharon was a bastard. Nobody appeared to be exactly certain of her father's identity, but whoever he was, somebody's chromosomes had suddenly run amok, and the product of this rebellion was the mysterious Nordic beauty which belonged to Sharon. This sort of thing was not unusual in India, but when it did occur its importance to the life of the person involved could hardly be exaggerated. Years later, I was convinced that Sharon owed her life to that magnificent red mane and those green eyes.

Had she been born with dark hair and a coffee-coloured skin, I think she might well have been left to die in a ditch, instead of being brought up by her aunt, when she was discarded by her feckless gypsy mother. I now know that her life was an example of the debris left in the trail of the British Empire. She was one of the losers, a casualty washed up by the great tides of colonial expansion.

The shabby saga of her life, and those of her forbears, was not at all uncommon even in those days, when the power of the British Raj was dissolving with terrifying rapidity. Her grandfather, Angus Carter, a genuine Englishman – whiter than white, so to speak – had come to India as a member of the Bengal Pilot Service. According to the legend, and I am sure that most of it may have been pure fantasy, he was the product of an aristocratic family which was both extremely rich and closely connected to the cream of Belgravia. But after he had been in the country only a couple of years, destiny confronted him with a plump, smiling Anglo-Indian woman who had already been married twice. Unbelievably, he not only fell in love with her but proposed, marriage, and in doing so instantly committed social suicide. I think now that he must have been an extremely stubborn character, a natural rebel, who refused to conform to the conventions of his own country, or those of India. As the years passed, his withdrawal from life became increasingly apparent, and eventually he moved his few possessions into this shabby bungalow skulking in the heart of a noisy bazaar. In these surroundings he succeeded in producing two daughters, and getting an overpowering addiction to alcohol. I gathered that he was a very tall bony man, well over six feet, with a small head, a long nose and a crop of fiery red hair. His manner was dictatorial and he never allowed it to be forgotten that he was a member of a family born to the purple. His eldest daughter was the woman I now knew as Miss Carter, and the other was Sharon's mother.

And then, some time in the early twenties, he became involved in a calamity which destroyed what was left of his life. One dull morning, with the monsoon rain pouring out of a leaden sky, the ship he was navigating down the Hoogly, struck a sand-bank, and was soon a total loss. The crew got off without difficulty, but in due course Carter had necessarily to appear before a Marine

Court of Inquiry to answer a charge of culpable negligence while on duty. He protested his innocence with passionate conviction, but after the Court had learnt that he had consumed three quarters of a bottle of whisky early that same morning, their verdict was predictable. He was found guilty and instantly dismissed from the Pilot Service. He died six years later, dragging out this remnant of time in a twilit world clogged with frustration and defeat. During those last years, his drinking increased, and he spent the greater part of his time sprawling on a low planter's chair, staring apathetically into the dusty courtyard beyond the veranda.

It was then that his second daughter – I gather that she was about sixteen at the time – got herself involved in a feverish love affair with a man whose identity was never clearly established. According to one version, he was a Welshman named Dorian Evans; another claimed that he was an Englishman from Bath named Parker. Whatever the truth may have been, it is certain that a child was produced from this union, or unions, and that this infant was subsequently named Sharon, and became the girl who was to play such a significant role in my life. Soon after Sharon's birth, her mother disappeared with yet another man, and the baby was left to the care of her elder sister.

I find it almost impossible to write objectively of Sharon. I loved her so much, owe her so much, that it is difficult not to forget the flaws which undoubtedly existed below the surface of her generous, carefree personality. But even when I loved her most I never blinded myself to her capacity for destruction, her genius for involving herself with the most unsuitable men, and thus bringing havoc to everybody with whom she was connected. I suppose that I could say that I loved her not so much in spite of her intransigencies, as because of them. She was destined to remain in my life for nearly seventeen years, and at the end of that time, despite her many infidelities and the humiliation she brought me, a bond had been forged between us which neither betrayal nor familiarity could break. She was to prove a steadfast friend, blind to my many weaknesses, tolerant of my repeated failures, always there to encourage me with her unfailing faith and optimism. We had been together for over seven years when the entire structure of my life was shattered, and during those dark months her love and belief were certainly responsible for saving my reason. And I owe her a hundred other debts. When my luck was out, my fortunes at their lowest ebb, she was capable of selling the clothes off her back to ensure that I had food to eat and a roof over my head.

Sexually, her presence in my life was essential. Like an addiction, each passing year increased my need for the delights that she alone could give me. I knew many other women, but in the end I always returned to her with the conviction that nowhere else could I find the complete fulfilment, the perfection of love which she could bring me. Yet it is also true that she frequently deserted me, became involved with new, short-lived loves which temporarily left me aching with pain and loneliness. After a while I became accustomed to these aberrations, realizing dimly that they were inseparable from her restless, instinctive response to life. Now, when it is all over, the lovers forgotten, suffering and humiliation blurred by time, all that is left is the memory of an enduring love that in some strange fashion remains both beautiful and indestructible.

Her many forays, her repeated infidelities, now seem of little importance. All I can remember is that she could laugh with the spontaneous innocence of a child, that she was fearless and compassionate, with a capacity for love that was unique. I remember the hundred times she lay in my arms on my untidy bed, her long graceful legs gripping my body, smiling with unutterable satisfaction as the rites of love achieved a climax.

In fact, when I recall the beginning of our relationship, it seems astonishing that it should have survived at all. I realize now that during those early years I behaved with a selfish stupidity that defies belief. I would leave her without compunction, sometimes for a period of several months, whenever a new job or a fresh adventure sent me on my travels. I took everything I could from her without offering her marriage, or even accepting the vaguest responsibility for her future. I would leave Calcutta for weeks, sometimes months, and expect to find her waiting for me on my return, and for the first couple of years I was never disappointed. But then without warning or apparent reason, the pattern changed. I would get back to a silent house in which Sharon's laughter and her loud expressive voice were no longer audible. When I questioned her aunt, her answers were evasive and slightly embarrassed. It did not take me long to discover that Sharon had found a new love during my absence, and I was astonished at the tides of rage and jealousy which this knowledge produced. We would quarrel furiously, and she would always promise never to leave me, and would then repeat her treachery all over again.

Overlapping those tempestuous developments, I was also searching for and finding fresh outlets and new loves. These included a Turkish call-girl, named Yasmin, tall and graceful, who I discovered, when it was almost too late, was not so much interested in my sexual prowess, or any other endearing traits I might possess, as in obtaining a British passport. There was also Jenny Page, a torch singer, and a very bad one, who insisted on singing to me at the most unlikely moments, in a voice of extraordinary power and disharmony. There were many others, even more bizarre, nourishing tastes which covered the entire gamut of sexual experience. But none of these lasted for more than a matter of days, or, at their most protracted, a few months.

Those were the years when the need for exploring the varied facets of love gripped me with a force that I was totally unable to resist. Although I expended hundreds of hours experimenting with the grotesque, darker tides of desire, it was always Sharon to whom I eventually returned. Every other kind of love was a caricature, a meagre substitute for the ecstasies which Sharon alone could produce.

This was the period, some time early in 1939, when I first attempted to become a writer. I had nourished this dream for almost as long as I could remember, and now I felt that to postpone it any longer would be both cowardly and unwise. I bought myself a large book bound in a limp red cover, an enormous bottle of green ink and a cheap fountain pen, and got to work. Every night, as the rain poured down with melancholy determination and Sharon lay dozing across my bed, I settled down at my clumsy, untidy table and strove to translate the tenuous stuff of my dreams into words. Outside my room, a gutter, filled to overflowing, gurgled and spluttered incessantly. I would work for hours at a stretch, sometimes long past midnight, until at last pure fatigue, or Sharon's querulous complaints, forced me to desist. Every morning I would read what I had written the night before to Sharon, who would listen enthralled, with a mixture of awe and affection which was extremely flattering to my ego. She, at least, was firmly convinced that I could have matched both Tolstoy and Dostoevsky without the slightest difficulty and, as always, her confidence inspired me to continue my efforts long after I was secretly convinced that I was totally incapable of creating a single sentence of real value.

And then, sometime towards the end of the war, Sharon began to change. It was as though she had suddenly become aware of all that she had missed in a material sense during the years that lay behind, and was now determined to get her share of life's luxuries. At last she told me that she had accepted a proposal of marriage from a man much older than herself, named Rees-Williams. I heard this news with a sensation of severe pain which was not entirely based on selfish considerations. The man she had chosen was a Master Mariner, employed by a large shipping company, and I did not think he was likely to bring her anything resembling permanent happiness. For one thing, he had been married twice before; for another, I detected a vein of sentimental egoism in his character which I instinctively distrusted. His appearance, too, was far from prepossessing. He was short and tubby, with a fleshy round face and a pair of dark, cunning eyes. In contrast to his rotund upper portion, his legs were extremely thin and bony, and as he was addicted to wearing knee-length socks and stiffly creased shorts which flapped about just above his knees, the effect was slightly ridiculous. All the same, I had to admit that his movements lacked neither agility nor energy, and he was capable of leaping upon various items of furniture to change a fused bulb, or adjust a faulty blind, with the speed of a mountain goat. He appeared to have a great deal of money, and it was rumoured that most of this wealth was due to the skill with which he smuggled the occasional packet of heroin past the Customs. I knew that Sharon did not love him, and I tried to warn her that the prolonged intimacies inseparable from a marriage, no matter how affluent, could prove a great deal more irksome than she visualized. But for once, nothing I could say would induce her to change her mind. The Captain presented her with an expensive engagement ring and soon afterwards installed her in a de luxe flat facing Chowringhee.

In due course they were married, and necessarily, the demands of a new, opulent life made it increasingly difficult for me to see her. From my point of view, the consequence of all this was to increase the loneliness and frustration which now became difficult to ignore. My sister Mary had already left India and my father was deeply engrossed in winding up his business interests preparatory to joining her in England.

The cool weather had started, and outside my room the sun, robbed of most of its power, shone day after day from a cloudless sky; but I seldom left my dark room, and the knowledge that I was soon to be deprived of my last real friend, with nothing ahead but the prospect of facing a changing, hostile India, was anything but pleasant. And then, late one afternoon, as I sat dishevelled and unshaven, slouched over my table, struggling to write my sluggish novel, Sharon slipped through my doorway for the last time. She was due to start her journey to Bombay on the following day, and once there, embark for England.

She came towards me as she had done hundreds of times before, and at first I looked at her with a vague resentment, a thrust that was very like hate. She was looking extremely well, and because she now had all the money she needed, her clothes were both expensive and elegant. She told me of her plans, and for the next few minutes neither of us seemed able to think of anything to say. She stood looking down at me, her face oddly inscrutable, her eyes apparently hard. And then, all in a second, the real implications of everything this visit implied struck home, and I was conscious of the impact of a pain so severe that it was as though an artery had been severed. This moment of agonizing clarity seemed to pierce both of us simultaneously. As I rose to my feet, she stepped forward, and in another instant we were clinging together with a desperation that was almost animal. Her face softened, her lips partially opened, and as I stood looking into those beautiful green eyes, I saw that a solitary tear was sliding down the smooth pallor of her face.

This wild embrace was not so much sensual, as an expression of almost childlike fear and despair. We both knew then that what had happened was tragic and unnecessary. The memory of all those long years we had shared burnt like fire, and as I tasted the salty flavour of her tears on my lips – for now that first tear was but one of many – the conviction that we could never be happy apart, and that this ridiculous marriage was both futile and doomed to fail by every conceivable law, tore us apart in spasms of misery and regret. I cannot remember exactly what was said during those last few minutes; the words were unimportant. All that mattered was that even while we exchanged tears and incoherent sentences, I was sure that our story was at an end and that we should never meet again.

My forebodings were justified. Just three months after she had left India, I received a brief note from my sister telling me that Sharon was dead. I never did learn all the details, but it appeared that the car in which she was a passenger was cut down by a tanker, somewhere on the outskirts of Birmingham. It was little consolation to be assured that it was almost certain she died instantaneously.

15

My first, vague intimations of disaster must have occurred some time late in 1938. It all happened so long ago that I can't now recall exactly where I was at the time. It might have been Mysore, Hyderabad, or even Madras. The truth is that I was moving around so fast in those days that the exact locality has become buried in the debris of the past. And yet what I do remember is as vivid and distinct as a strip of film hidden inside my head. It is morning, and I am standing before a small, round mirror preparing to shave. Behind me is an untidy bed and a table supporting a teapot, a greasy plate, and a cup still partly filled with tea. I am sure that I am in some sort of hotel, but for the life of me I can remember neither its name nor its exact whereabouts. There is the sound of crows cawing from the dusty compound outside, and a shaft of bright sunlight slants through an open window. Beyond my room, in what I suppose must have been either the hall or dining room, my ears pick out the soft pad of bare feet and the subdued murmur of voices.

My cheeks and chin are covered with lather, but as I grip my razor and bend forward to focus my slightly absurd reflection, something attracts my attention and my finger moves involuntarily upwards to touch my forehead. About an inch and a half above my right eyebrow a small reddish lump is visible. It seems slightly larger than a sixpence, and it appears to glow like a hot ember. I didn't much like the look of it and yet I am sure that this small discoloration did not worry me for more than a few seconds. My body, my physical well-being, was the one thing that had never failed me yet, and I possessed the illogical conviction that it never would do so. Heaven knows, I had called upon it often enough to perform feats which should have destroyed it years before. I had never taken the trouble to feed or care for it adequately and yet the damn thing seemed to have secret resources of strength and resilience which were always available. I could talk and drink all night, fall into bed utterly exhausted at 5 a.m., and still wake just three hours later, relatively refreshed and capable of going to work, and then repeat the process all over again.

There was also another reason for my inexplicable failure to react to this danger signal. At that time I was living as a wanderer, seldom sleeping in the same bed more than twice, perpetually harassed, always on the move across the vast, impassive expanse of India.

I had got myself a job as a salesman with a crooked American firm calling itself Masterpieces Inc. The representatives of this organization swarmed across the country in big, fast cars, devouring all those who were gullible enough to become their prey. Goaded forward by a bulky American boss named Pat Hogan, our ragged crew – known by the way as the Spartans, to differentiate it from several similar teams – worked its way purposefully through the lesser known regions of southern India.

We penetrated Secunderabad, Bangalore, Hyderabad, Mysore, and a dozen other forlorn isolated cities. For the first time in my life I glimpsed the secret heart of India, and the experience was somehow extremely unnerving. In these areas the influence of the European seemed barely visible, and the relative insignificance of our role was only too apparent. I could drive for hours through a huge, crowded city, submerged in its mysterious, alien life, and never see a single white face. I had lived in India for most of my life but I learned more about the country in those few, feverish months than I had learned in all the preceding years.

It did not take me long to realize that in joining Masterpieces Inc. I had got myself involved with a gang of particularly loathsome crooks. I had become a 'Picture-man', and as such could now claim to be amongst the elite of high-pressure salesmen. Pat Hogan, his gold teeth flashing in a wolfish grin, would constantly proclaim, 'To sell pictures you've really got to have what it takes, because we all know that in fact what we're trying to sell is not worth a pig's turd.' Their racket was simple but effective. Using a special glib spiel, which we were compelled to learn by heart and ferociously enjoined to deliver without changing a single word, we persuaded our victims to purchase, at exorbitant prices, coloured enlargements of family photographs. These portraits when delivered were enclosed in an ornate gilt frame behind convex glass, which gave them a deceptively attractive three-dimensional appearance. Thus, our prey were not only forced to pay a colossal fee for the enlargement, but in due course were confronted with yet another bill for the gilt frame, without which the reproduction instantly dissolved into nothing more impressive than a large limp photograph.

My career with Masterpieces Inc. was an inglorious mixture of failure and absurdity. Apparently, I lacked the ability even to become a successful crook, and as week followed week without my being able to bring back the essential orders, Mr Pat Hogan's disapproval became increasingly vocal. Finally I was sentenced to the ultimate humiliation, and while all my companions roared through the city in big, expensive cars, I was relegated to an ancient phaeton drawn by a bony, underfed horse. In this vehicle, travelling at a funereal pace, I would lurch laboriously through the sun-baked streets as my fellow salesmen shot past me with the speed of arrows. This did little to help my vanity, but I was soon on the best of terms with the old Indian coachman who drove this equipage, and would frequently turn to him for help and advice.

I could easily fill this book with all I saw and did during the course of these wanderings, but what matters is that all this time, without knowing it, I was moving closer and closer to the single terrible moment when the entire structure of my life was to be destroyed. It was in yet another unknown hotel or rest house that I once more noticed that small, ugly lump. Again it was morning, and I was standing in an untidy room struggling to put on my tie. As always I was in a hurry, harassed by the pressures and uncertainties the day was sure to produce. I pushed my head forward, staring at my reflection in the mirror, and as I did so I realized that the lump I had seen earlier had been joined by another small swelling which exactly duplicated the first. Some days later these two lumps joined together, forming a single unsightly eruption which appeared to glow, crimson and sinister as though lit by some mysterious heat. Now for the first time I was conscious of real anxiety. I didn't like the look of that lump at all, and despite my instinctive dislike and distrust for doctors, I decided then and there that the time had come to enlist their aid.

But this was not as easy as it seemed. I was working then somewhere on the outskirts of Mysore, and I was fairly sure that it would be almost impossible to find a European doctor in our vicinity. I consulted my old coachman and he listened to my story with patient understanding. At last he said reassuringly, 'I know a pukka Tamil doctor fully qualified and deeply experienced, who can certainly help you.' The next afternoon we plodded slowly into a part of the city I had never visited before. At last we came to a halt in a small sandy square surrounded by a weary assortment of small shops and grimy old houses. The coachman pointed to a peeling, green door on which the name Dr Sundala Venketaram was painted. I pushed open the door and found myself facing an old, flabby man, grey-haired, and wearing a rather dirty collarless shirt. He seemed half asleep, but as I walked forward his eyes opened, and he pulled himself erect. He motioned me to a shabby chair, and leaned forward across his desk studying my face. I pointed to my forehead, explaining when the lump had first appeared and adding that as it showed no signs of disappearing I had now become really troubled. As I spoke, he kept nodding his head. 'Yes,' he said, 'of course; I understand; exactly.' And as his lips moved, his stubby brown fingers probed and stroked the skin on my forehead. After a couple of minutes he pursed his lips and emitted a reassuring sound. 'It is nothing,' he said confidently, 'just scar tissue. It will disappear in a matter of weeks.' I wanted to believe that he was right and he seemed so certain of his diagnosis that I handed over five rupees and left his room feeling relieved and happy.

I did not worry about the mysterious swellings after that, but tried to forget that they were there. This conviction of immunity must have lasted quite two months, and then a third signal of disaster sprang at me one evening in Madras. I realized then for the first time that this was one catastrophe I was not going to escape.

I had left Masterpieces Inc. by then, and was living in a down-at-heel hotel on the outskirts of the city. I remember that I had been asked to a party and was busily engaged in getting myself into my only presentable suit. It was not much of a party, but because it was sure to provide food and beer, not to mention several pretty girls, I was looking forward to it eagerly. I had a bath and then pulled on a clean blue shirt, before climbing into my trousers. For a moment I was naked, except for the shirt flapping against my thighs.

There was a long glass directly behind me, and as I swivelled around and prepared to pull on my trousers, I caught a fleeting glimpse of my bottom in the bright surface of the mirror. In that fraction of a second I saw that there was on my left buttock something which resembled a large, circular bruise rather smaller in size than the palm of my hand. It did not look particularly ugly or threatening, and yet I was instantly conscious of a current of fear and repulsion. I let the trousers fall, and screwing my head around attempted to view this puzzling discoloration over my right shoulder. But I discovered that simple anatomical laws rendered this feat impossible and after a few seconds of ineffective acrobatics I stepped backwards towards the glass. Now I was in a position which allowed me to study this mysterious mark at my leisure. I thought at first that I must have bruised myself in some way, but this explanation seemed less satisfactory when I realized that I felt no pain however hard I pushed my fingers against it. I spent several minutes twisted around, staring at the thing in bewildered fascination. I couldn't understand it, but I was now convinced that something was dreadfully wrong.

But I was an irrepressible optimist, and did not find it excessively difficult to forget this sinister incident for the rest of the night. The next day I consulted yet another doctor. In this case I selected a young Scot with thinning hair and a ginger moustache. He examined my forehead, and then the patch on my bottom carefully, but I got the impression that for a while at least he was completely mystified. Then his expression cleared, and he lifted his head and faced me with a confidence born of complete certainty. 'Food poisoning,' he said authoritatively, 'you've been eating some muck from the bazaar, and it's got into your system. Don't worry, I'll give you something which should clear it up fairly soon.' He scribbled a prescription, gave me a brief lecture on the necessity of watching my diet, and accepted two ten-rupee notes with practised nonchalance.

Once again I was reassured. I swallowed his pills diligently, and waited for the marks to disappear. But despite the drugs, they were still visible three months later when I returned to Calcutta, and various fresh, inexplicable symptoms had made their appearance.

The palm of my right hand became strangely numb and severe nerve pains shot down the entire length of my arm. The marks on my face were now prominent enough to attract attention, and after a while I became used to the question 'What the hell have you done to your face, Greave?' Within days of my arrival in Calcutta, unwilling and filled with premonitions of disaster, I made my way to the Skin Department of the Medical College Hospital.

This hospital, huge and grim as a medieval fortress, was situated deep in the heart of the Indian city. Fate had apparently decided that this vast ugly labyrinth of a building was to play a significant part in my life. I had been born inside one of its ancient, huge rooms, and twenty-one years later had almost died there of paratyphoid. During this second encounter the entire structure had almost been destroyed by the worst earthquake that Calcutta had experienced for a hundred years. I remember lying in bed, watching in fascinated horror as the ceiling swung from side to side, and suddenly the grey surface of the walls was split by a deep, uneven crack which stretched from the ceiling to the floor. After all this, I was more or less convinced that the place could hardly surprise me again; but I was wrong.

I must have reached the Skin Department of the hospital some time in the early afternoon. After a delay of well over an hour, I found myself seated at a desk facing a young Indian doctor. He was good-looking and assured, with dark, alert eyes, and a smooth, fair skin; somehow I knew instantly that here was a man who really understood what he was doing. He took me in at a single, swift glance, and I thought that his eyes suddenly narrowed as he studied my face. He asked me when I had first noticed the lumps, and when I told him it was nearly a year ago, his expression remained inscrutable. He appeared to reflect for a minute, and then said gently, 'I am going to ask you to close your eyes, after which I'll touch your face with this piece of cotton wool. Tell me when you feel it against your skin.' His nimble brown fingers closed around a fragment of cotton. As I obediently closed my eyes, I could feel him dabbing delicately first at my forehead, then my cheekbones, and finally my jaw and neck. 'Yes, yes, yes,' I said, as I felt the faint pressure of the cotton wool moving across my face, and it seemed to me that I was reacting with complete precision to the movements of his exploring fingers. After this operation had continued for several minutes, I heard his voice, reassuring but firm. 'Right; that will do. You can open your eyes now.' As I did so he lowered his head, and a few seconds of silence ensued.

When at last he spoke his voice was persuasive but authoritative, and he was smiling almost as though the two of us were about to share something which was slightly absurd and amusing. 'Now,' he said smoothly, 'you must realize that you need not consider what I am about to suggest as anything more than a precaution. There is no necessity for you to feel unduly worried, but I do think that it might be advisable for you to go to the Leprosy Department, and let them test you.' Involuntarily my head jerked up as I stared at him in horrified amazement. But as he continued to assure me that such a test was most unlikely to be positive, and that its major objective was merely one of elimination, my instinctive reaction of terror was gradually replaced by something approaching confidence.

It took me fifteen minutes to find the Out-Patients' Leprosy Department. It was hidden away in a distant corner of the building almost as though the authorities wanted to keep its existence concealed. I don't remember how I felt as I fumbled my way forward down numerous dark corridors, because suddenly both my surroundings and myself had become strangely unreal. When I reached the threshold of the Out-Patients' Department I discovered that I was not eligible to enter this delectable region until I had been alloted a hideous pink card, covered with very small, almost illegible print. The Leprosy Department consisted of a single large, shabby room which adjoined a series of smaller cubicles into which the patients were ushered one by one to confront the waiting doctors. The larger room smelt of sweat, unwashed bodies, and another odour, cloying yet bitter, which permeated the entire section.

As I passed through the door, I realized instinctively that I had crossed a frontier from which I could never return. The room was crowded with thirty or forty Indians, and as I looked at them a cold tremor washed through my body. Most of these people were outcasts, beggars, the dregs of a great Indian city. Many of them were almost naked, a few were horribly mutilated and disfigured. They gazed towards me without astonishment, and one or two of them even smiled with a vague friendliness which seemed to say, 'Welcome brother; you are one of us now.' In this world all were equal, and I had to wait my turn in a long, patient queue.

I recall two small incidents from this period of inaction. A young Bengali of the student class drifted into the room. A certain indecision of movement and the smooth, unmarked surface of his youthful face indicated clearly that he was merely a visitor, and as I glanced at him I was suddenly aware that the man's eyes were glazed with terror. He picked his way across the floor, shuffling nervously, circling around the others, shoulders hunched, his face stiff with fear. After he had covered a few yards, his right hand gripped the folds of his spotless dhoti and lifted it upwards so that he was able to cover his nose with the soft, white fabric. And then I saw a young Indian girl, slim and graceful, eyes downcast, facing one of the doctors, and something in the sad resignation on her face told me that she too was a victim of this shameful scourge. Eventually I found myself in the presence of a small, middle-aged rather fleshy Indian doctor. His well-fed face observed me with detached curiosity. 'We will have to take a nasal smear,' he said, his voice falling into the cadence of a rich chee-chee. A wisp of cotton bound around a thin length of stick was inserted delicately into each of my nostrils, and I was told to return the following afternoon to hear the result of the test.

I don't know how I spent the rest of the day. I'm quite sure that I didn't get drunk, and I know that I avoided talking to anybody else about my predicament. The result of the test was still to come, but even then I was almost certain that my luck was out. During that long evening and night, and all through the next morning, I did not read or listen to music, but just sat in a chair while my mind strove to accustom itself to fresh vistas of horror.

The next afternoon at exactly 2.30 – I recall that the bazaar was bathed in radiant sunlight – I found myself again in that hateful room staring into the face of the plump Indian doctor. He was standing beside his desk wearing clean white overalls, flanked by two young Indian doctors who had probably just qualified. His eyes refused to meet mine, and after a slight pause I heard his voice, matter of fact, utterly detached, say, 'When would you like to start treatment?'

I was determined to drag this thing out into the open once and for all. I forced him to meet my eyes, as I asked with a dreadful imitation of composure, 'What exactly is wrong with me, doctor?' Again his eyes slid away from mine, and he said briefly, 'You are suffering from leprosy.'

As those terrifying words hung in the air, I caught a glimpse of the face of one of the young doctors. His dark eyes were lit by the horror that should have belonged to me, and I knew instantly that this was a man capable of compassion and understanding. This flash of awareness was to play a significant part in the years that followed.

I asked just one more question, 'Can it be cured?' I heard myself saying it with grotesque, prim formality, and the plump doctor replied jovially, 'Why not? Why not?' I agreed to attend the Out-Patients' again the following day to start treatment, and I did not realize until I was back on the crowded street that he had not answered my question.

*

The disease was diagnosed on the eleventh of August 1939; it is one of the few dates that remain permanently in my memory, and the Second World War came just twenty-three days later. It was a dull, rain-drenched evening, and I stood on my small veranda, staring gloomily down at the damp asphalt of a narrow, deserted road. I had been an acknowledged leper for just over three weeks, but still failed to accept or even completely believe it. I was scruffy and unshaven as I leaned over the parapet, and all I can remember about my thoughts at that moment is a grey cloud of boredom and frustration. Suddenly the street was filled with shrill cries, and half a dozen Indian newsboys loped towards me, brandishing a special edition of *The Statesman* and shrieking 'War declared – War declared,' again and again. The crows fluttered into the air and in a matter of seconds the entire city seemed to explode into unexpected life. I listened to these sounds with blurred detachment. My world had been so recently destroyed that it hardly seemed surprising that everything which was familiar and secure should also be shattered into fragments.

A great deal had happened since that afternoon in the Out-Patients' Department. I visited the hospital twice a week to receive the agonizing injections of Chaulmougra oil which was then the only treatment available. The marks on my face had already begun to improve slightly, but the scars of horror and revulsion which lay hidden inside my mind were not so easily cured. I had become afraid, shrinking from leaving my room, dreading the long uncomfortable journey by tram to the hospital gates. I am quite sure that I would have given up even the pretence of attending the clinic had it not been for Sharon's unfailing courage and sympathy. She would accompany me on these journeys, chattering loudly to distract my attention, threading her arm through mine when my footsteps faltered as we approached that sinister objective. I do not doubt that without her presence I would have succumbed to the temptation of suicide which, in those early weeks, constantly obsessed my thoughts.

A few days after the diagnosis, news of my predicament was brought to my father, and he, no doubt reluctantly, agreed to let me have a monthly allowance of three hundred rupees paid through Lloyds Bank. This, in view of our prolonged estrangement, was indeed generous, and it is only fair to record that he continued to support me for the next eleven years. Three hundred rupees was not enough for luxuries, but in the India of those days it was more than sufficient to guarantee food and shelter.

I booked a small room and prepared to adjust myself to a new, twilit, fugitive world. A small, stocky Nepalese boy brought me my lunch every day, and in accordance with my doctor's advice I lived for the next six months on a purely vegetarian diet. I hardly ever left my room, but Sharon was with me through each long scorching day, often remaining at my side until the darkness had been replaced by the grey pallor of dawn. Gradually the gap which divided me from the life and friends I had known before became increasingly wide. And then I struck on a plan which rendered further visits to that gruesome clinic no longer necessary. Doctor Mukerjee, the young Bengali whose face had expressed such sympathy on that fateful afternoon, agreed to visit me weekly at my room, and there give me the complicated and painful injections which were considered essential. He was to continue treating me for over ten years, and though we were never to become intimate, his instinctive compassion never failed to impress me.

The years which followed were full of fear and unrest. As the war dragged on the city changed, pulsating with a new feverish life. Thousands of soldiers slouched through its streets, jeeps and huge army lorries driven at breakneck speed forced pedestrians to scamper to safety. In due course, the Americans appeared, and now each flight of steps and street corner had its quota of lanky, gum-chewing GIs. Everything throbbed with a strange, rather horrifying vitality. Seedy bars and nightclubs spawned and multiplied, the nights became hideous with the clamour of jazz bands and the jagged turmoil of drunken laughter. Sex and hysteria swept across the city like the waves of an incoming tide. As Japanese bombs fell on the crowded bazaars, our local girls pranced and postured with the abandonment of voodoo dancers.

I watched all this with numb curiosity, slipping like a shadow through the dark, noisy streets, absorbing everything but never attempting to participate.

At that time I knew very little about the infection which had so effectively ravaged the course of my entire life, but with the passage of time I could not help learning some of its secrets; and as my knowledge of it grew, I became increasingly proficient at separating the real facts, which Heaven knows were terrifying enough, from the vast mass of ignorance and misconception which like a nightmare permeated every aspect of this subject. At the end of it all, I was left with the bitter conviction that a very great proportion of all the suffering it has produced was based on nothing more substantial than the stuff of bad dreams and irrational terror.

Leprosy has afflicted the human race for more than five thousand years, and when I think of this enormous span of time, a picture, vivid and compelling, forms in my mind. I see a great multitude of outcasts, a thousand ragged, lost battalions, stretching back through the ages, until they disappear below the curve of time. It seems impossible ever to calculate the hundreds of thousands of hearts this merciless disease has broken, the agonizing loneliness and misery left in its wake.

Mankind has suffered under countless scourges, many of which are much more lethal and painful than leprosy, but they differ in one significant, all-important characteristic. Cancer, syphilis, cholera, multiple sclerosis and a score of others bring death and destruction, and yet they do not evoke the terror and revulsion produced by leprosy. In contrast to the onslaught of these others, leprosy makes no effort to conceal its ability to mutilate and disfigure, but rather inflicts its sentence with an insolent disregard for human sensitivity. Because its handiwork is so clearly visible, its victims, since time began, have been branded as outcasts and subjected to every possible form of psychological and physical cruelty.

The ironic and pitiful fact is that we now know that almost all these fears were unnecessary. I was speaking recently to an international authority on every aspect of this disease, and he summarized the basic facts: 'Leprosy is the hardest disease to catch, and the easiest to cure.' Careful and prolonged research during the past thirty years has proved that eighty per cent of the entire human race cannot contract the disease under any circumstances whatever, and the remaining twenty per cent can only succumb if they are brought into close and continuous contact with it in its infectious state. With the help of modern medicine, this danger is greatly reduced as the disease can now be rendered non-infectious in a matter of weeks. If it is recognized early, a cure can generally be guaranteed in quite a short time.

Unfortunately it cannot be denied that leprosy, particularly in the Third World, is not decreasing, though I have been assured that if funds amounting to the relatively small sum of sixty or seventy million pounds were immediately available to assist preventive medicine, this ancient curse could be completely eradicated within two or three generations. It is interesting to learn that the Biblical version of this disease which has done so much to make people hold it in special horror, bears no resemblance to the disease we now identify under that name. In other words, it seems certain that, in the past, thousands of unfortunates were subjected to the ultimate in degradation when in fact they were not suffering from leprosy at all.

About six months after that grim afternoon in August, I moved into a larger room on the ground floor of a peeling tenement. This room had no windows, so that it was necessary to burn the electric lights throughout the day and night. Perhaps this explains the fact that, when I think of those years now, all I can remember is darkness. This is odd, because I must have lived through hundreds of days of dazzling sunlight; but all that remains is the memory of darkness, a big dark room filled with shadows, blue spirals of cigarette smoke drifting towards the ceiling, and the sound of my voice arguing interminably as I faced the dim figures seated on the other side of the table.

I could feel the disease, like a cunning enemy, gradually gaining strength as each restless month passed. I was living like a fugitive, a criminal, and I had come to this place in search of seclusion and anonymity. Instead, I soon found myself involved in a new kind of life, fresh, unexplored and intoxicating. My love for Sharon sometimes achieved ecstasy, though it more often submerged me in humiliation and despair, and I formed deep friendships with the other inhabitants of this hidden, twilit world. One of them was a young Anglo-Indian, educated at a public school in England, who had the face of a Hindu ascetic.

His heavy-lidded eyes, finely chiselled aquiline nose and compressed lips gave him an expression of melancholy introspection, and he certainly possessed an intelligence which was both unusual and impressive. He lived only a few hundred yards from my door, sharing his lodgings with a slim brown girl named Antoinette. She was quite exquisitely beautiful, with high cheekbones and huge black eyes set at an oblique angle. But she had had polio as a child and one of her legs was an inch shorter than the other, forcing her into an ugly shuffling limp. Then there was a hunchback, a young Sikh educated in Germany, nervous and temperamental, who wrote poetry which frequently evaded even his efforts to understand it. These people and various others became accustomed to visiting my room several nights a week. Soon after midnight, as I sat reading at my untidy table, a soft, unobtrusive knock would sound on my door, and when it was opened they would slip across the threshold to remain talking through the rest of the night.

In the meantime, concealed but implacable, the disease continued its work of destruction. Some time in 1942 I lost the sight of my right eye, and almost immediately the other eye became severely infected. I suffered weeks of excruciating pain, wincing uncontrollably whenever the pupil was exposed to light. Eventually even the flicker of a match as I attempted to light a cigarette produced a second of pure agony, forcing me to duck my head swiftly as though avoiding a blow. This pain was often so severe that I could not sleep and spent the long, dark hours walking backwards and forwards across my room, drugged with half a dozen codeines. When I told my Indian doctor of these symptoms he listened patiently, his long brown face expressing genuine concern; but he was nothing if not truthful, and all he could say was 'There is nothing we can do.' In the end I developed a primitive method of relieving the pain for myself. I would fill a large bottle with hot water and then press the warm glass against my closed eye. This gave me momentary relief and I would often spend several hours sitting motionless pressing the slippery bottle against my face.

I cannot deny that those eight long fugitive years plumbed depths of terror and pain which I can never forget; but it is true to record that they also gave me moments of happiness, interludes of razor-sharp awareness which illuminated everything I did with a special radiance. Because I was living on borrowed time, even the smallest achievement brought with it a sensation of indescribable satisfaction and joy. I am sure now that I lived with an intensity and zest during those dark, hidden years which I can never capture again. Love, friendship, fear and pain, fused with each other to produce an intricate pattern of light and dark. I knew that I was playing a losing game, but the certainty that my time was running out made each second precious and beautiful.

The war ended at last, but I knew that for me life would only become more difficult. Now the communal hatred, repressed during the course of the war, burst free with savage force. The city was torn apart with blood and terror. Everybody admitted that the British Raj would soon disappear, but nobody could guess what was likely to replace it. Riots, assassinations and strikes became the order of the day. It became unsafe to venture out at night, and every day the papers carried fresh stories of murder and arson. My room was robbed twice in a single month. I came back to find the place a shambles, empty drawers and broken chairs flung across the floor. The thieves had certainly done a thorough job; not only all my clothes but even my mattress, pillows and sheets had been removed. Worst of all they had taken an expensive portable gramophone lent to me by my sister, and for no apparent reason half a dozen of my diaries and notebooks. This incident was repeated a few weeks later, and this time the robbers even removed the bulbs from the light sockets.

My sight had become so bad that I only dared face the sunlight when my eyes were concealed behind dark glasses and at night I was almost completely blind. My small Indian servant deserted me, Sharon had sailed from Bombay, and my father too was preparing to leave India to join my sister Mary in England. Everything familiar and reassuring was slipping away from me and there seemed nothing I could do to escape the moment of ultimate disaster. In August 1946 the city exploded in a fresh wave of murder and terror. Great mobs roamed the streets killing and destroying everything they saw. There were nights when the darkness was slashed by the light of a score of huge fires, and the vultures became gorged with their diet of human flesh. The city smelt of fear and decay. My doctor was compelled to stay away, because I lived in a Moslem quarter and he dared not risk his life on the streets.

And then, one morning late in 1946, when I had almost forgotten the taste of hope, a limp, airmail letter was thrust beneath my door. It had been posted in London and was written by a Doctor Riley. I read the dim typewritten page with incredulity, and for several minutes failed to understand its meaning. But at last my brain started to function, and as I gradually understood the significance of those blurred words, hope returned like a long-lost friend. Dr Riley's message was simple and direct. In some inexplicable fashion he had heard of my plight, and was now writing to press me to come to England, where, he assured me, I could depend on both treatment and care. I realized that if I missed this chance I would certainly never be given another. I read the letter through several times, and instantly my mind began to think and plan with savage speed. The letter, arriving when it did, was like a miracle, but I realized even then that many obstacles must be surmounted before it became a reality.

Now, new pressures and fears replaced the old familiar phantoms which had haunted me for so long. I wrote and received letters, held long discussions with my doctor, checked the cost of steamship passages and sailing dates from Bombay. Planning my escape was a slow, frustrating process. As I succeeded in overcoming one obstacle, its place was taken by half a dozen others. Because British rule was soon to end, the task of leaving India was fraught with many difficulties. Thousands of British troops still remained in India, and the necessity of transporting these men home greatly reduced the number of civilian passages. In those early days I had no clear idea of how my voyage to England could be arranged. The possibility of travelling in the ordinary way seemed too unlikely to merit serious consideration, and when I did consider this difficulty I could only conclude that it would probably be necessary to send me over on a hospital ship or, possibly, a specially chartered aircraft.

I did my best not to look too far ahead, and forced myself to contend with each new obstacle as it appeared. Dr Riley asked to see a detailed copy of my medical history from the date when I first started treatment. This involved several weeks of anxiety and delay before the essential documents were collected and put in the post. Then came another moment of unexpected triumph. I received yet another letter from Dr Riley, and I could hardly believe my eyes when I read that he had no objection to my booking a normal passage. He wrote, 'Your medical notes clearly indicate that you are now completely non-infectious, and accordingly I have no hesitation in advising you to travel in the ordinary way.' Until I received that letter, I do not think I really believed that all my efforts were much more than a kind of complicated game, but once I read that sentence the last remnants of doubt were put to flight.

I had not seen my father for several years, but now I wrote him a note suggesting a meeting at the first possible moment. I met him late one evening in his flat, high above the street, overlooking Dalhousie Square. He listened to my story in silence, his face expressing chill disbelief. When he did speak, his voice was soft but without warmth. 'I don't see the point of it all,' he said at last, carefully avoiding meeting my eyes. 'What will you do when you get to England? I mean, what do you expect to achieve by travelling half way across the world in your condition?' But I refused to accept defeat. I pointed out that once I reached England I could get the latest treatment, and that Dr Riley had guaranteed my admission into a hospital designed specifically for the care of lepers. In the end, unwillingly and with something that seemed very close to hostility, he capitulated. He pulled out his cheque book and wrote the necessary words with careful distaste. I remember that after I had thanked him I caught a fleeting glimpse of his face as I walked quickly towards the door. He was staring after me with impassive concentration, as though he never expected to see me again, and I still do not know whether pity or mere boredom lay behind that blank, unrevealing gaze.

16

I had been with my father rather less than half an hour, but it was completely dark when I returned to the street. I hailed a rickshaw which took me straight to Thomas Cook's, and fifteen minutes later, with the odd sensation of playing a part in a dream, I had booked my passage on board the *SS Franconia* scheduled to leave Bombay on the tenth of August. Several months had to elapse before that date, months of indescribable anxiety, but at last the morning of my departure arrived. When I awoke, the first thing I saw was my large black trunk, packed and locked, glaring at me like a challenge. The morning was dull and grey, and everything that happened seemed oddly sluggish and unreal. I stood on the veranda, staring down into the dusty compound, and was unreasonably depressed by the fact that everything looked exactly the same. Half a dozen monkeys sat disconsolately on the low yellow wall which separated us from the next house. Scores of these animals had escaped from the zoo during the panic and disorder of the Great Killings, and had long since become a familiar part of our surroundings. A young Indian lay on his side, sleeping peacefully on the path beside a bed of wilting flowers. Crows fluttered from the roof-tops to perch on the branches of a leafless tree. There was no sound except the distant roar of traffic plunging down an invisible street. The phantoms of the past drifted across my mind like shadows.

I remembered standing on this same veranda that evening, long ago, when the Japanese planes first bombed the city. I had been terrified, but Sharon, still in her pyjamas, had insisted on hurrying into the street, determined to get as close as possible to the scene of the disaster. I recalled the sight of her, exuberant and confident, hurrying up the flight of steps which led to the flat. So much of my past lay trapped inside that unkempt garden that it was difficult to realize that it must soon become nothing more tangible than a ghost from the past.

Finally, when my trunk and suitcase were neatly stacked near the landing above the stairs, I said goodbye to the Nepalese bearer who had served us for so long. He stood in front of me stocky and impassive, belly sagging, hair streaked with grey, and I remembered how different he had looked sixteen years before when we first met. I gave him twenty rupees and my old German air rifle, which I knew he had coveted for a long time, and for a moment his old face became alive and happy. Miss Carter displayed no emotion as we said our farewells. Her small glazed blue eyes stared into mine with the resignation of a lifetime composed of partings and defeats. She had been discarded so often that the treachery of existence had lost the power to surprise her. When I told her that she could keep my few scraps of furniture, her small eyes opened momentarily to express a vague, greedy satisfaction. I could think of nothing to say. I hugged her clumsily, and in another five minutes my luggage and myself were moving in a decrepit red taxi towards the station.

As the taxi moved swiftly down the long, clear sweep of Chowringhee, I drank in my last view of the city with greedy curiosity. I loathed and feared the place, and yet because it had consumed the best part of my youth I could not help but love it at the same time. Wherever I went, whatever happened to me, the memory of every inch of that tumultuous, vociferous street would remain inside my memory. I had passed down it ten thousand times, in the blazing sunlight, through the hot sweltering darkness, in the half-light of dawn and the dusk of the evening. Now, as I raced through it for the last time, it seemed more crowded and menacing than ever before. Great crowds drifted past the shops and hotels. The city appeared to be bursting with restless, uncontrollable life. A few minutes later we were crossing the ugly yellow river, thrusting its way seawards in a stream of liquid mud. I glanced down at it from the ramparts of the bridge, and for some reason remembered how, thirty years earlier, when I was still a child, I had seen the corpse of a man, his white dhoti still billowing above the water, drifting beneath that bridge towards the sea.

Although the boat train was not due to leave for another hour, it was already almost full when I reached the station. A harassed mass of passengers and porters hurried past the long line of chocolate-coloured coaches, searching for a compartment which they could claim as their own. I found myself a bunk somewhere near the rear of the train, shoved my huge box under the seat, and let myself relax temporarily on the hard cushions.

The days of the journey dragged endlessly. Twelve hours after we had left Chowringhee, one of the small electric fans gave up trying, and soon the confined space stank of sweat and urine. After the first day, the compartment became increasingly messy and uncomfortable. Open suitcases lay on the seats flanked by piles of soiled clothing. To reach the corridor, one had to step over a collection of discarded tea cups, which had been left on the floor and remained there until the end of the journey. I sweated and suffered as the hours dragged slowly past. I wanted to remain as inconspicuous as possible, but one of my companions, a young Scot, noisy and assertive, seemed determined to render this impossible. A few hours after we had left Calcutta he actually managed to involve me in a ridiculous game of whist. He had unwisely chosen to become my partner, but after my obvious ineptitude with the cards had cost him several rupees he wisely decided to eliminate me from further play. But he never stopped talking for a second, and his endless questions and barely concealed efforts to learn my business soon produced a sensation of pure claustrophobia. Finally, goaded beyond endurance, I snarled, 'Mind your own bloody business,' at which he rose angrily to his feet and pushed into the corridor, knocking over one of the tea cups as he did so.

My mind had plenty to occupy itself with. I could not forget that for me this journey, and what would come afterwards, was fraught with a score of sinister possibilities. It was like an amputation. I had cut myself free from everything that represented security and peace and now, branded like Cain, was gambling my life on an unpredictable adventure. Like a man touching a sore tooth with the tip of his tongue, I could not prevent my mind producing a succession of fresh disasters. After all, I had no guarantee that I would ever get as far as boarding the ship. I knew that I would have to confront some sort of medical examination and if this proved to be more than a mere formality I might easily be detected and turned back when I was within a few feet of the ship. If this happened my journey back to Calcutta would indeed be hazardous. British rule was due to end in a matter of days, and it was generally believed that the entire country would explode yet again, in another outburst of communal killings. I knew only too well what such a climax might involve.

I pictured myself marooned in Bombay, slinking through the dark streets, surrounded by howling mobs and the smoke of a burning city. In that event, trains might easily be no longer available. And the task of returning to my base nearly two thousand miles away would become indescribably difficult. Even if I succeeded in boarding the *Franconia* there were still other dangers. Life on a ship was necessarily cramped and exposed; I would have to undress in a crowded cabin, bathe and shave in a washroom used by scores of other men. I could not conceal the marks on my face and arms, and consequently detection, accusation and disaster might occur at any moment. My imagination created a hundred fresh possibilities of exposure.

I remember that on the last evening, as I sat watching the countryside float backwards through the window, the thought came to me, 'Look hard, drink it all in, because this is your last sight of India.' All I saw was a brown featureless plain stretching away to the extreme limits of the horizon. There was no colour, no beauty, just the scorched earth under the bright sunlight, and a single tiny mosque, like a grimy white bubble, staring at me across the flat landscape.

Early the following morning the train reached the outskirts of Bombay, and we were gradually swallowed by the great city. The train slowed as it passed a level crossing and just for a moment I got a clear view of the faces huddled together behind the peeling gates. There were poor Indians, factory workers, coolies, representatives of the voiceless millions which constituted the mass of the country. They stood there, in the early morning sunlight, and I could feel the terror and madness which pressed down on them like an unbearable weight. Small brown, bony men wearing dirty shirts and torn trousers peered at the train, their eyes glazed with fear, their faces pinched and despairing. It was easy to believe that I was watching an era die, and that the future for all these people held nothing but uncertainty and terror.

The train ground to a halt under the shadow of a huge warehouse. The sea, smooth and green, was visible beyond the cranes on the wharf. The passengers scrambled out onto the dusty platform like a pack of mangy wolves. Watching them as they milled around in the clear, early sunshine, I thought that I had seldom seen an odder assortment of grotesques and misfits. It was as though the dregs of an empire were being poured out of a dirty bottle, and it was little comfort to realize that I probably fitted only too well into this ragged company. Strange swarthy faces, their eyes wary yet innocent, peered nervously around them, expostulating and complaining in the liquid chee chee that must have belonged to a score of forgotten cantonments.

Eventually the passengers began to drift more or less aimlessly through the doorway that led into the huge warehouse. In contrast to the brilliant sunlight outside, everything was now enveloped in a blue twilight. The ceiling was very high, and a shout or a loud voice produced a hollow reverberating echo. Great stacks of luggage, mounting thirty or forty feet above floor level, were tended by gangs of coolies. I found myself in an endless queue, shuffling slowly forward towards some invisible point.

I was now confronting the ordeal which I had dreaded for so long, but the extraordinary fact was that I was barely conscious of fear. Everything seemed a shade unreal, as if I were an actor who had rehearsed the scene too often, but my mind was unusually alert and perceptive. There was no point in anxiety or fear, because from now on I could do nothing to change the course of events.

The long dispirited line moved sluggishly through the gloom. We would shuffle forward half a dozen steps, pause, then shuffle forward again. For perhaps fifteen or twenty minutes I could not see what was happening at the head of the queue, and then at last I glimpsed three men huddled together over a large desk. A naked bulb hung directly above them, so that their faces and the upper halves of their bodies were clearly visible in a pool of hard yellow light. The central and dominating figure in this group was a plump, trim little man of about fifty. He had a round, pink face, greying hair and a large, full-lipped mouth which seemed parted in a perpetual grin, but his eyes were alert and confident. In contrast to him, the man on his left, also European, had a long cadaverous face with bushy eyebrows, and a look of bored suspicion. The last member of the trio was an Indian, presumably a doctor, a short wiry man, brisk and efficient, who constantly lifted his head to scan his surroundings with restless curiosity.

I took them in with the fatalism of a prisoner confronting the judges who have the power to decide the entire course of his life. I was relieved to notice that they seemed eager to get through their share of the formalities. Each member of the queue was dealt with rapidly and, as far as I could judge, with nonchalant indifference. His passport and vaccination certificate were scrutinized briefly by three separate pairs of eyes, the passport was stamped by the man in the centre, and a new supplicant moved forward.

The examination seemed to last about ten seconds, and the men at the desk hardly glanced at the faces passing before them. Consequently, when at last I found myself facing the three inquisitors, I was feeling relatively confident and optimistic. I handed over my passport, never doubting that it would be passed down the line in the usual fashion, but what actually occurred was so unexpected that, for the first few seconds, I was only conscious of a sensation of shocked bewilderment. Instead of glancing swiftly at my passport and pushing it towards his companion, the plump little man held it between his fingers for a moment, and then placed it, still unopened, on the desk. I followed his movements with hypnotic concentration. He leaned far back in his chair, half suppressing a yawn, while he appeared to study me attentively through his inquisitive brown eyes. I felt myself suffocating in a wave of pure terror. And then he smiled with good-humoured irony, almost as though we were conspirators sharing some private joke. His right hand moved towards his breast pocket, and emerged grasping a packet of cigarettes. Very slowly he opened the packet, extracted a cigarette, and placed it between his lips. Still watching me, he started to fumble in his trouser pockets, presumably in search of matches. But at this point the Indian doctor suddenly produced a lighter, and lit the cigarette. The entire process could not have lasted more than half a minute, but when it was over and my passport had been returned, my face was clammy with sweat.

And now, like a pack of lemmings, the crowd began to move. I was carried forward by the momentum of hundreds of jostling, scrambling bodies. I had to struggle to remain on my feet, and as bony elbows prodded my ribs and hard shoulders collided with my own there was no time for congratulation or relief. Suddenly we emerged from the warehouse, and swarmed onwards, blinking owlishly in the sunlight. Directly in front of us, high and steep as the flank of a cliff, rose the bulk of the *Franconia*. Packed into the crowd of passengers, I only knew we had reached the gangway leading upwards from the wharf to the ship when the shuffling of our footsteps changed to a series of crashes as we scurried across the iron floor plates. Beyond the gangway, a low steel door, like a dark hole in the side of a hill, led into the cavernous interior of a lower deck. Two petty officers, sleek and efficient, ushered us through this opening with the speed and precision of collies herding sheep. And then, like an electric shock, my brain started to function again, in an unforgettable moment of triumph and astonishment.

I pushed myself against the wall, pulled out my handkerchief, and began to mop my face. It was difficult to believe that at long last I was on board, and that the first lap of my escape had already been achieved. Abruptly the silence was shattered by an inhuman roar, as the loudspeaker above my head burst into grotesque life. An enormous grating voice began to sing, 'Now is the hour when we must say goodbye.' After a couple of minutes, I moved uncertainly forward, climbed a broad stairway and found myself on the upper deck. The rails were lined by hundreds of passengers, craning their necks, shouting farewells to their friends and relations on the wharf below. I found an empty niche close to the stern of one of the lifeboats, and stood looking down.

The *Franconia* was already free and drifting ponderously a hundred yards from the dock. The deck under my feet tilted slightly as the great engines came alive and the screws started to revolve, churning the water astern into a torrent of foam. Now the ship began to move purposefully forward, thrusting its bows against the small green waves. I stared at the vanishing city with an odd mixture of love and distaste. I saw the graceful arch of the Gateway to India become gradually small and indistinct, and remembered that I had been there when it was still being built. I turned my head and saw, on the other side of the harbour, the shadowy outline of the island of Elephanta, and I realized with a pang of vague sadness that I had never visited those mysterious caves, and now I never could.

After a while the other passengers began to move away and go about their various errands. A gang of seamen worked their way along the promenade, clearing away the debris of our embarkation, and disappeared. A gong sounded to summon us to a meal. The deck was now quite empty, but for a long time I stood there alone, leaning on the rail, watching the shoreline drift imperceptibly into the distance, until at last India, and my youth, had been obliterated by the curve of the wide, anonymous sea.

More About Penguins and Pelicans

Penguinews, which appears every month, contains details of all the new books issued by Penguins as they are published. From time to time it is supplemented by *Penguins in Print*, which is our complete list of almost 5,000 titles.

A specimen copy of *Penguinews* will be sent to you free on request. Please write to Dept EP, Penguin Books Ltd, Harmondsworth, Middlesex, for your copy.

In the U.S.A.: For a complete list of books available from Penguins in the United States write to Dept CS, Penguin Books, 625 Madison Avenue, New York, New York 10022.

In Canada: For a complete list of books available from Penguins in Canada write to Penguin Books Canada Ltd, 2801 John Street, Markham, Ontario L3R 1B4.

Recent and Forthcoming Penguin Titles

The Mint

T. E. Lawrence (352087 A/c Ross)

That Lawrence exerted a strange hold over men's imaginations (on which he capitalized) there is no doubt. His reasons, therefore, for throwing up everything after the creation of the Arab States, and seeking the anonymity of the R.A.F. barrack-room, are difficult to understand.

Some of the answers are supplied in *The Mint* which, as he wrote to E. M. Forster, was 'a private diary, interesting to the world only so far as the world may desire to dissect my personality'. It is also a superb example of Lawrence the writer as it brings to life with appalling, if poetic, precision and clarity all the harsh and often unpalatable realities of men living together.

This edition includes a Preface by J. M. Wilson

Dictionary of Fairies

Katherine Briggs

'A magnificently researched, illustrated directory of fairies of the British Isles. There are entries on assipattles and mumpokers, on fairy dress, on fairy crafts and food, and, most useful this, on spells to obtain power over these fiendish Little People. It is so entertaining that I would rather recommend it as a bedside companion than as a serious technical reference book' – Selina Hastings in the *Daily Telegraph*

Recent and Forthcoming Penguin Titles

Jonathan Cape, Publisher

Michael S. Howard

'A portrait comparable to Arnold Bennett's bookseller in *Riceyman Steps* . . . the very model of a model Cape biography' – Michael Holroyd in *The Times*

'A gorgeous plum pudding of a book stuffed with publishing stories' – Tony Godwin in the *Listener*

The Life of Bertrand Russell

Ronald W. Clark

An eloquent and intimate biography of one of the most significant figures of our time. Born into the high world of the Whig aristocracy, among people for whom Waterloo was still almost a personal memory, Bertrand Russell lived to inspire the campaign against nuclear warfare. Ronald Clark provides a fascinating and graphic portrait of the man, and there is virtually no aspect of Russell's long life to which something new is not added by this remarkable book.

'A major work of research' – Philip Toynbee in the *Observer*

Three Guineas
Virginia Woolf

Those who consider that Virginia Woolf was too wrapped up in her art and set to take notice of what went on around her, will be confounded by this witty, elegant and lucid polemic, which so magnificently argues the case for sexual equality and for women's liberation.

Far from being a rarified treatise on Bloomsbury's notions of 'literature', *Three Guineas* was rather an extremely pertinent and well-aimed opening shot in the battle which still rages today.

The Decline and Fall of the Middle Class
Patrick Hutber

Unfashionable, unpopular, hard to define, the Middle Class is on the run, staggering under the twofold impact of taxation and inflation. Yet nearly half the people in this country consider themselves to be in this category and they are angry about the erosion of their standards.

Patrick Hutber shows exactly what is happening, and points out what can be done to reverse the decline. His book is not simply a plea, but a serious warning. If the Middle Class disappears society as a whole will suffer for it.

'A pithy, well-written survey' – *Sunday Telegraph*

To be published in Penguins

The Book of Cats

Edited by George MacBeth and Martin Booth

P. G. Wodehouse's Webster, Saki's Tobermory, Kipling's Cat that
Walked by Himself, Eliot's Macavity, Don Marquis' mehitabel:
short stories from Patricia Highsmith, Roy Fuller and Giles Gordon:
the classics of Walter de la Mare, W. W. Jacobs and Edgar Allan
Poe: the cats of Robert Southey, Théophile Gautier and Theodore
Roosevelt: the observations of Aldous Huxley, Henry Fielding and
Mark Twain: and paintings by Bonnard, Goya, Picasso, Chagall,
Hockney and Douanier Rousseau.

In all, a rich, affectionate medley of prose, poetry and picture,
assembled by George MacBeth and Martin Booth, in praise of that
most elusive and fascinating of creatures – the cat.

The Face of Battle: A Study of Agincourt, Waterloo and the Somme

John Keegan

'A brilliant achievement ... In this book, which is so creative, so
original, one learns as much about the nature of man as of battle'
– J. H. Plumb in the *New York Times Book Review*

In this provocative, revelatory book, John Keegan takes issue with
the traditionalists – the conventional historians to whom ordinary
soldiers are ciphers, and who present battles as encounters between
generals and states, not between people.

The Face of Battle is military history from the battlefield: a look at
the direct experience of individuals at the 'point of maximum danger'.
Without the myth-making elements of rhetoric and xenophobia,
breaking away from the stylized format of battle descriptions,
John Keegan has written what is probably the definitive model for
military historians. In his scrupulous reassessment of three battles,
he manages to convey their reality, and their significance for the
participants, whether facing the arrow cloud of Agincourt in 1415
or the steel rain of the Somme in 1916.

To be published in Penguins

The Life of Noël Coward

Cole Lesley

'*The Life of Noël Coward* is – to borrow Coward's own description of his life – "fabulously enjoyable": a graceful and glistening piece of biography, reading which is like a holiday in a rented Rolls' – Kenneth Tynan in the *Observer*

'Funny, sad, witty, bawdy and totally unputdownable, it sheds new light on its many splendoured subject and enshrines for all time several decades of social history. I loved it!' – Peta Fordham in *The Times*

In Vogue : Six Decades of Fashion

Georgina Howell

In Vogue encapsulates the history of twentieth-century fashion in Britain.

In Vogue is not just fashion in its narrower sense of women's clothes; but fashion in its wider context seen influenced by social and cultural attitudes, by literature, by the visual and performing arts, captured with all the customary *espièglerie*, perception and wit for which *Vogue* is famed.

In Vogue builds up a composite picture of the woman, year by year, from her hair to her shoes, to her scent, her stance and her cut of clothes. Here, too, are the women that wore them – Theda Bara, Lady Diana Cooper, Gertie Lawrence, Vivien Leigh, Audrey Hepburn, Twiggy – and the designers who dressed them – Poiret, Vionnet, Chanel, Dior, Mary Quant, Saint Laurent – and the artists who projected the image – Steichen, Beaton, Horst, Bailey, Eric and Bouché.